Our Peculiar Times

Also by George William Rutler
from Sophia Institute Press:

A Year with Fr. Rutler

Stories of Hymns

Hints of Heaven

Grace and Truth

George William Rutler

Our Peculiar Times
Catholic Wisdom for Times of Crisis

SOPHIA INSTITUTE PRESS
Manchester, New Hampshire

Dedicated to the memory of
Eric Lionel Mascall

Contents

Introduction

When Sir Alexander Fleming studied cultures of staphylococci in 1928, he was looking at what had been around before there were people to measure time, but he took time to study a common mold as something uncommon. That is how we got penicillin. What may have saved more lives than any other discovery was always there, waiting to be discovered. This I would propose as a metaphor by which to analyze the events of the day. The wisdom and stupidity that edify and deface the human condition have been active or latent in every generation, but only by our paying close attention to them can they be effective examples and warnings.

In this interest, I submit the following collection of recent essays that appeared originally in *Crisis Magazine*. They were written in a time of unusual social challenges. "May you live in interesting times" is an ironical phrase usually assumed to be a curse. There is an added irony about it, since it is commonly thought to be of ancient Chinese origin, but in fact it probably was introduced there in the 1930s by the British ambassador extraordinary and plenipotentiary, Sir Hughe Montgomery Knatchbull-Hugessen. Consistent with my theme, there are no uninteresting times, so long as one pays attention. But our times may be singular for their lack of perception, being the result of widespread ignorance about how people dealt with challenges in the past.

Our Peculiar Times

This is why I have made frequent, even possibly profligate, use of historical references to help put things into a balanced perspective. Occasionally, I have also engaged subjects that may seem to offer no vital significance to issues at hand, although they are not meant to be mere "divertissements," and I hope they are not without some moral application to current circumstances. If I wander at times, I summon to my defense Terence: "Humani nihil a me alienum puto." When it comes to writing in general, Terence's broad appreciation of topics for conversation inspired the first female playwright, Hrotsvitha of Gandersheim (935–973), and modern literati such as Montaigne and Molière and even John Quincy Adams. So the present crop of postmodern writers does have precedents.

The pandemic of 2020 began as I finished this collection. Its consequences, and those of other unpredictable events, whatever they be, may be analyzed better by using the method of close attention, which makes all times interesting.

—GWR

The Bondage of Cultural Illiteracy

We could have a summer of love.

— Jenny Durkan, mayor of Seattle

"At last I am free!" declared Martin Niemöller, holding a small book as the prison door was locked behind him. He had been allowed to keep a Bible, and his words would have been an inscrutable paradox only to those who do not understand the freedom ensured by literacy, and the greatest freedom endowed by words that are sacred.

After the destruction of the Second Temple in AD 70, the Jews relied on literacy to preserve their culture, with the Mishna as the written record of what until then had been an oral tradition of rabbinic commentaries. While practical illiteracy seems to have been common, every male attained full manhood by reading some lines of the Torah. When the Living Word became flesh, He asked at least four times: "Have you not read . . . ?" (Matt. 12:3, 5; 19:4; and Mark 12:26). On the very day of the Resurrection, He asked the two men on the Emmaus road why they did not understand what the prophets had written. Later, the obviously well-lettered official of the Ethiopian royal household was reading in his chariot when he encountered Philip and learned what Isaiah meant.

The first part of the Eucharistic Liturgy is the "synagogue part" because the synaxis teaches from the Sacred Books. "For I delivered to you as of first importance what I also received, that Christ died for our sins in accordance with the Scriptures" (1 Cor. 15:3). Since the transmission of knowledge and its ancillary wisdom is fragile and dependent upon faithful stewards, civilizations require civilized people strong enough to defy barbarism. The most morbid way to destroy the moral integrity of people is to deny and obliterate awareness and comprehension of their history. In *Brave New World* Aldous Huxley wrote, "Almost all human beings have an infinite capacity for taking things for granted." To take the artifacts of a civilization for granted is an almost-absolute guarantee that they will be lost. There is much more evidence for that than just the winds blowing over ruined Angkor and Timgad, and forgetting them proves the point. As Belloc contemplated Timgad while visiting Algeria, he mused: "The Barbarian is discoverable everywhere in this, that he cannot make: that he can befog and destroy but that he cannot sustain; and of every Barbarian in the decline or peril of every civilization exactly that has been true."

Romans commonly had Greek slaves as teachers, because they were better educated than themselves. This actually gave the slaves an advantage, as Horace sardonically admits: "Graecia capta ferum victorem cepit et artes intulit agresti Latio — 'Conquered Greece captivated her uncivilized conqueror and brought her arts into rustic Latium.'" In Scotland in the eleventh century, King Malcolm did not bother to learn how to read, for warriors expected clerics to do that for them. But he was charmed by the way his wife, St. Margaret, could read to him; and the subjects she chose helped to direct the course and shape the customs of her adopted land. Malcolm took pleasure in decorating books for his lady, and one of them, bound in gold and silver, is preserved in the Bodleian Library in Oxford. Margaret was an Anglo-Saxon, born in exile in Hungary. She could read Latin, which served as the international language of culture much the way English is used in air traffic control towers around the world today. The power of the written word explains why Nat Turner's Rebellion in 1831 was followed by anti-literacy laws in all southern states except Maryland, Kentucky, and Tennessee. Frederick Douglass learned how to read and write secretly and would prove his own dictum: "Knowledge is the pathway from slavery to freedom." Because "new occasions teach new duties," as the abolitionist James Russell Lowell hymned, on the day I am typing these words I am taking computer lessons from two African American friends of mine, who are as patient with me as Margaret was with Malcolm.

Many were surprised in 1953 when President Eisenhower—in an eloquent commencement speech at Dartmouth, and without using notes or the yet-to-be-invented teleprompter—confounded his critics, who had caricatured him as inarticulate, by warning: "Don't join the book burners. Don't think you are going to conceal faults by concealing evidence that they ever existed. Don't be afraid to go in your library and read every book, as long as any document does not offend our own ideas of decency. That should be the only censorship." Having considerable experience of war, Eisenhower had seen the consequences of thought control. At the time, his warning was an oblique nod to the "Red Scare," which, we now know through the Venona Papers, certainly was not unfounded, but which invited the extremism of unstable figures.

Back in 1821 Heinrich Heine said: "When books are burned in the end people will be burned." The destruction of the great libraries of Alexandria by Muslims in 642 and Cluny by Huguenots in 1562 had irreparable consequences. So, too, with the mutilation of art in all its forms. It is not a question of taste or subjective aesthetic judgment: it is simply the fact that to rewrite history is eventually to resent history altogether, to live in the present without past or future, mocking the venerable and venerating pastiche heroes.

Our Peculiar Times

In such a cauterized atmosphere, demagogues deftly beguile blank minds with illusions. Goebbels turned the death of a problematic twenty-three-year-old Horst Wessel into a martyrdom, pretending that the sacrificial Aryan lamb had written his own "Horst-Wessel-Lied," sung as an anthem stirring enough to make millions march to doom, as did "The Internationale." Those well read in the annals of time will be aware that lies can sound like truths when sung to a good tune.

In 1984, George Orwell warned with chilling foresight of a dystopia in which records of the past would be destroyed or falsified, monuments of culture would be pulled down, and "nothing exists except an endless present in which the Party is always right." There is more than a whiff of that right now in burning cities, fostered by what is legitimately called "fake news" describing the ransacking of part of Seattle as a "summer of love." The mayor of Seattle said that the violent occupation of part of her city was a congenial block party, in the way the illiterati might call the Normandy invasion a happy day at the beach. The cruelest illiteracy consists in a pantomime education that commands what to think rather than how to think, and erases from a culture any memory of its tested and vindicated truths. Technological literacy easily becomes a camouflage for cultural illiteracy. I have witnessed youths flee from a room at the sound of a Mozart sonata; the same youths enjoy vulgarities sung to discordant sounds on the most refined acoustical amplifiers. In this I hope I am not merely a stubborn anachronism, and I even boast at not being shocked by novelties. But I was indeed stunned into uncharacteristic silence when I showed a film version of a P.G. Wodehouse novel to recent college graduates, who required subtitles because they could not understand the clipped English speech.

Cultural literacy can liberate from humbug, and there is a lot of that in selective indignation. Those who read enough may learn that self-conscious progressivism is often pompously regressive. As for racial taxonomy, it developed as a structured philosophy in the dark musings of some of those hailed as heroes of the so-called Enlightenment. John Locke provided protocols for slavery in *The Fundamental Constitutions of Carolina*, which gave slave owners "absolute power and authority" over their human chattel. In 1753, David Hume was "apt to suspect the Negroes, and in general all other species of men ... to be naturally inferior to whites." Immanuel Kant was confident that "humanity exists in its greatest perfection in the white race.... The Negroes are lower and the lowest are a part of the American peoples." With exceptions such as Emmeline Pankhurst, leaders of the women's suffrage movement carefully segregated their parades. Carrie Chapman Catt promised, "White supremacy will be strengthened, not weakened, by women's suffrage." The first statue of a woman in the Capitol's National Statuary Hall, contributed by Illinois, is of Frances Willard, who complained that "the colored race multiplies like the locusts of Egypt." Of her meeting with the black sculptor Edmonia Lewis, Willard noted: "She is ... unusually good-looking for her race, though she has its salient characteristics of physiognomy and voice." Woodrow Wilson simultaneously endorsed women's suffrage and Jim Crow laws.

Absent the restraints of classical humanism, and contemptuous of its moral cadences, eugenics moved racism into the laboratory. In London, a bust of Marie Stopes remains unscathed along with a copy of the love poems she sent to Hitler in 1939. Margaret Sanger approved and encouraged the German sterilization program of physicians including Dr. Josef Mengele. There was public indignation when the Catholic Church became the most strident opposition to the eugenics crusade by invoking her tradition of culture. When

Our Peculiar Times

Jesse Jackson was a significant leader, he called abortion "black genocide," and, at the March for Life in 1977, he asked: "What happens to ... the moral fabric of a nation that accepts the aborting of the life of a baby without a pang of conscience?" But his political career required that he move from literacy to illiteracy, and in 1987 he joined another march at Stanford University, chanting: "Hey hey, ho ho, Western culture's got to go!" Decadence takes only a decade.

Wisdom that comes from literacy requires a special agency of grace to distinguish the fake news from the good news whose Author asks each generation: "Have you not read ...?"

June 23, 2020

Who Will Guard the Guardians?

Six or seven centuries "are like an evening gone" when tracing the course of common sense, and so James Madison found no anachronism in conjuring the shades of Juvenal and Cleon, more than six centuries apart, to make a point about the perils of the right and wrong manipulation of human will. He asked with Juvenal, *"Quis custodiet ipsos custodes?"* The dilemma—who will guard the guardians?—was the same dilemma that conflicted the Athenians during the Peloponnesian War, back in the fifth century BC, when their better instincts for peace were compromised by the seductive propaganda of Cleon. In this thesis, Madison was joined by Hamilton and Jay in *The Federalist Papers*, which were not expected to be the daily reading of farmers and merchants, but which could easily be understood by them and anyone bound by human nature. The matter at hand was "a rage for paper money, for abolition of debts, for an equal division of property." That rage resulted in Shays' Rebellion and occasioned reflection on mob rule.

People can indulge contrary instincts to riot or to stay calm, because their will is free to do so. It is a principle denied by those who excuse moral anarchy by saying, "The devil made me do it." That is the theological version of the behaviorist's impulse to blame disordered behavior on external influences.

9

Our Peculiar Times

The rage now inflaming our cities is taking place between Pentecost and Trinity Sunday, although it is unlikely that those enraged are liturgically sensitive to that.

Celebration of the Most Holy Trinity follows Pentecost because it is through the Holy Spirit that the sublime truth of God as Three in One expands the limits of human intelligence. The perfect harmony of the triune God is like music whose frequency cannot be registered by unaided hearing, but reverberates in the systematic order of nature, evident in those things we take for granted: health, happiness, and peace.

The peace that Christ gives is not a human fabrication (John 14:27). But as the Creator has entrusted the care of His creation to humans as His most complex creatures, we are responsible for promoting what St. Augustine called the *tranquillitas ordinis*—"the tranquility of order."

When the human mind works in harmony with the indications of the Holy Trinity, great things can be accomplished. For example, this past week two astronauts on the SpaceX craft docked perfectly in outer space. In a devilish irony, this was accompanied by rioting in our streets, nihilistic in its destructiveness. As many of the bomb throwers and arsonists were middle-class suburbanites turned terrorists, this was a commentary on the collapse of family life and the abandonment of serious education in the schools, but essentially it was a specimen of the misuse of free will. Among millennials grown dependent on forces that suborn conscience, who have never outgrown the need for a nanny, 70 percent favor socialism and one-third see something hopeful in communism. The desecration of St. Patrick's Cathedral with graffiti was not a display of adolescent erudition in the etymology of four-letter words rooted in German cognates and Old French. It was the screech of young people who for various reasons and from various sources had come to think that the Divine Word of Life is an incomprehensible whisper.

Who Will Guard the Guardians?

It is my lot to be the pastor of a parish in the middle of my city's riots, just as New York has been an epicenter of the viral pandemic. Last night a shop next door was attacked. My parish has had a long experience of mobs, and the city records claim at least thirty-four riots of significance. The first pastor of my parish, who served for thirty-four years, intervened in the 1863 Draft Riots to save a Presbyterian church nearby from burning, an act that anticipated the modern ecumenical movement but with more practical benefits. His efforts were not permanent: later in his tenure, in 1873, the Orange Riots nearby saw sixty-three killed. Just days ago, I watched Macy's department store being boarded up, to little effect, since looters with impunity used crowbars to break in and steal jewelry and other expensive things in what much of the media said was an expression of their desire for social justice.

By the careful orchestration of mobs, and the systematic delivery of bricks and bats, it was clear that sinister plotting was at work, and that our president was right to call it terrorism. Not every authority was as acute. Our mayor, Bill de Blasio, who for years has functioned like one of Job's unhelpful condolers, said he was proud of his daughter, who was arrested as a rioter. Governor Andrew Cuomo said in a CNN interview: "Those were not thugs and looters. These are young people who still have idealism and want to make this nation better. And that's a good instinct, and it should be encouraged." From our hierarchs, there has been little in the way of prophecy, save for occasional virtue-signaling bromides. But that is the consequence of a gradual emasculation of their moral influence. So far, our prelates have not emulated the three archbishops of Paris—Denis-Auguste Affre, Marie-Dominique-Auguste Sibour, and Georges Darboy—who were killed in 1848, 1857, and 1871, respectively. Affre and Darboy died in riots, while Sibour was shot by a cleric who thought celibacy was an imposition. All wore the same pectoral cross.

Our Peculiar Times

This week, as a church burned behind him in Washington, D.C., one television reporter, reminiscent of Iraq's famous "Baghdad Bob," insisted that there was no burning and that the "protesters" were peaceful. The disinclination of so many governors, mayors, and other social guardians—along with the media—to acknowledge that their perception of reality is unreal brings to mind W. E. B. Du Bois and Walter Duranty, who called Joseph Stalin "a great man" and "the greatest living statesman." This is much like George Bernard Shaw's panegyrics on Mussolini and Hitler, and John Kenneth Galbraith's immoderate flattery of Mao Zedong.

Those not averse to objective reality still have voices. The president of the New York State Troopers Police Benevolent Association, Thomas Mungeer, in a genuine protest, said that Governor Cuomo had given his men "zero support." He explained to Cuomo: "Peaceful protesters do not arrive with hammers and Molotov cocktails, burn police cars, smash the windows of businesses or spray graffiti on St. Patrick's Cathedral—criminal opportunists and vandals do. Peaceful protesters do not start fires in the streets or to businesses—arsonists do. Peaceful protesters do not gather en masse to openly disregard laws, create havoc and impede on the rights of the general public—rioters do."

So there sounds once again, whether in New York, Philadelphia, Dallas, Seattle, or any other city where the acoustics of tradition remain, the voice of Joshua along the Jordan: "And if it seem evil unto you to serve the LORD, choose you this day whom ye will serve" (Josh. 24:15, KJV). This week, the contrast between astronauts and anarchists is a model of the blessings and dangers of free will. "For the desires of the flesh are against the Spirit, and the desires of the Spirit are against the flesh; for these are opposed to each other, to prevent you from doing what you would" (Gal. 5:17). This simply and artlessly boils down to the choice between Christ and chaos, challenging the human mind to be rational or irrational. The human will is not bound to some arbitrary fate, but as John Milton put it: "The mind is its own place, and in itself can make a heaven of hell, a hell of heaven." It has been said one way or another that the gates of Hell are locked on the inside.

By choosing misrule, distorted reason prefers Hell to Heaven. The gates of Heaven are opened by choosing the tranquility of divine logic. "Behold, I stand at the door and knock; if any one hears my voice and opens the door, I will come in to him and eat with him, and he with me" (Rev. 3:20). To appropriate Rudyard Kipling, the destiny of souls depends on what people do with the "if" of their moral freedom: "If you can keep your head when all about you / Are losing theirs and blaming it on you."

June 4, 2020

Why Holy Week Is Holy

When a lady complained to the great short-story writer that her works "left a bad taste" in her mouth, Flannery O'Connor replied that what she wrote was not meant to be eaten. For the conventional palate, those often-macabre stories can be distasteful, but Miss O'Connor deliberately wanted to avoid the sentimentalism of much pious diction that eviscerated the sharp Catholic understanding of the human condition. That is why she could be acerbic about the parochialism that neuters Catholic apologetics. For her, "parochial" was the comfortable narrow-mindedness that suburbanized the Heavenly City and turned successors of the apostles into benevolent salesmen for annual charity appeals.

My one gripe with Miss O'Connor — and I parade it with a confidence born of the sense that deep down, she might actually agree — is that "parochial" is not a bad word if one really understands a parish. Actually, what is parochial is anything but parochial: *parochia* is an existence outside the confined dwelling, and you might say that it means "a family aware of more than itself." Use of it to mean "limited and narrow" goes back no farther than the mid-nineteenth century, according to the *Cambridge English Dictionary* (which, while not the *Oxford English Dictionary*, is reliable). The parish is an atom of existence, and everything in a parish,

15

from baptisms to burials and all the joy and grief in between, is a microcosm of life, which by its authenticity is more compelling than any fictitious comedy or tragedy.

No one is more parochial than a pastor, and the pastor of a parish in the heart of New York City is most parochial of all. The amiably mindless Bertie Wooster was amazed that the great thing about New York is that as soon as you get off the ship, you are already there. He may have had in mind my parish, whose canonical boundary extends to the middle of the Hudson River. Anyone drowning past that point must appeal to Newark.

These days, New York is the American epicenter of the viral pandemic; from a parochial point of view, my parish is the epicenter of the epicenter. As I write this, the USNS *Comfort* has just passed by, the same ship that was deployed the day after the attack on the World Trade Center. The Army Corps of Engineers has completed an "emergency field hospital," with a capacity for nearly three thousand beds, just down the street from my church.

I have just returned from my first day there. Where flower shows and boat shows and comic-book conventions were annually held, the scene has now become more somber. If this is parochial, such parochialism is as encompassing as the verses of Dante. That is true of most parishes everywhere, but the ubiquity of crises is part of Manhattan's cultural signature. In happy halcyon days, New Yorkers tend to trample on another, but in crises they are one. In 1992, my church on East Forty-Third Street burned down; then there were hurricanes and blizzards and power blackouts, and the carnage of September 11, 2001; and now this strange virus has emptied our streets. Having been part of all that, I think of Abraham Lincoln's eldest son, Robert, who was present at the deaths of three presidents; like him, I should not be surprised if society hostesses have relegated me to their B-lists.

Why Holy Week Is Holy

This is how we approach Holy Week, when the faithful observe the most important thing that ever happened. With a powerful shock this Lent, mortifications have not been freely chosen, but imposed by circumstances beyond human control. There is a strange silence; I suppose it is much like when the influenza contagion after World War I killed fifty million worldwide, the equivalent of two hundred million today. There is a picture in my rectory of the second pastor of my parish, who died at the end of the pandemic, having exhausted himself in ministering to the sick in the many tenements nearby. (I am the thirteenth pastor, but as a Catholic I am not a serious triskaidekaphobe.) During the time of the "Spanish flu," churches were closed. In Baltimore, Cardinal Gibbons complied with the imposed civil regulations, but objected that saloons and pool halls remained open.

Now everything is shut here, and the Passion will be more powerful because the veil of the Temple is drawn, and only a cry from the Cross can tear it open. The holy apostles thought themselves bereft of the One they had hoped might be the Messiah. On the Mount of Olives, three of them slept a depressed slumber haunted by anxious confusion. In every generation, various circumstances have given us the impression of being abandoned by the One who had promised to be with us always. Blaise Pascal wrote: "Jésus sera en agonie jusqu'à la fin du monde; il ne faut pas dormir pendant ce temps-là." (Jesus will be in agony until the end of the world. We should not sleep during this entire time.) The solemnity of those words was the freight of the confidence that tethers agony to victory.

In a book I wrote years ago, I remarked that modern communications have made popes more visible than ever, but a dangerous result is the impression that their significance issues from celebrity. Last Friday, Pope Francis stood in the dark and rain of a totally empty St. Peter's Square, and then blessed the whole world with the Eucharistic Lord. No scene in fiction could have been more poignant than the isolation of that moment. It brought to mind the dreary rain of the day Pope John Paul I was buried after his shockingly sudden death, prodding many to ask why this had happened to a man who had seemed a glimmer of hope just weeks before.

When Pope Francis was elected, there were naïfs who confused hope with optimism, and they expected a "Francis Effect" that would bring new life and vigor to a decaying culture. The decay has in fact worsened. Following some positive indications during the pontificate of Pope Benedict XVI, church attendance has dwindled, and so have seminaries and convents. Between 2013 and 2018, on all continents save Africa and Asia, priestly vocations shrank about 8 percent, and there are 52,000 fewer women religious and 4,000 fewer male religious as a result. But as Pope Francis stood alone in St. Peter's Square, which was as empty as many churches in the West, and the rain poured, there was a magnificent sound to the silence. It was as if the holy Voice was saying once again—this time, to a generation that has come to think of itself as a substitute for God and as lords of a New World Order whose shrines are in Silicon Valley and Brussels—"You have not chosen me. I have chosen you."

Without anticipating the present situation, I had written before that the real strength of the successor of Peter would be understood only when the millions of fans had melted away and the pope stood alone. The telecast of Pope Francis standing alone on March 27, in what is now called "real time," evoked the final scene in Robert Hugh Benson's dystopian novel *Lord of the World*. The antichrist would try to destroy the Church, attacking the lone figure of a pope exiled in Nazareth as he holds the Blessed Sacrament.

Why Holy Week Is Holy

On February 8, 1992, the future Pope Benedict XVI mentioned this book in a university speech in Milan, and he also quoted *Bonum Sane*, Pope Benedict XV's 1920 *motu proprio*: "The coming of a world state is longed for, by all the worst and most distorted elements. This state, based on the principles of absolute equality of men and a community of possessions, would banish all national loyalties. In it no acknowledgement would be made of the authority of a father over his children, or of God over human society. If these ideas are put into practice, there will inevitably follow a reign of unheard-of terror."

Pope Francis has called *Lord of the World* one of his favorite books, mentioning it in 2015 and before that in 2013 when he said that Benson described "the spirit of the world which leads to apostasy, almost as if it were a prophecy." Benson's dystopian novel would have a utopian sequel, *The Dawn of All*, which at least in style is inferior. The conclusion of the first book is ambiguous, and there is only a description of the antichrist about to attack the Vicar of Christ: "He was coming, and the earth, rent once again in its allegiance, shrank and reeled in the agony of divided homage."

The Victorian novelist Bulwer-Lytton wrote many fine things, and in fact was more innocent of prosaic lapses than Wordsworth. He is derided only because one of his lines has become a cliché: "It was a dark and stormy night." In ways that circumstance has yet to disclose, that dark and stormy night when the pope raised the Blessed Sacrament as the most parochial of pastors, with the whole world in his universal and immediate jurisdiction, was the harbinger of victory and not the whimper of defeat.

Now in the present contagion, Holy Week may seem to have been erased from moral conscience in an unprecedented way. A man in surgical mask and rubber gloves has just delivered our palms for Sunday, but we also have instructions that they are not to be distributed for fear of infection, and that there will be no public procession.

Let us give thanks for this fast and mortification of custom. This will be a great Holy Week because we are positioned to share the confusion and ambiguity of the crowds in Jerusalem when that enigmatic figure with a sublime countenance entered the city riding on a shabby beast. In days of shock and sorrow, He is calling attention to what in languid hours we may have taken for granted or possibly did not really understand at all—namely, why Holy Week is holy. Are the churches closed? Are the people quarantined at home? "I tell you, if these were silent, the very stones would cry out."

April 7, 2020

On Sport and Sacrifice[1]

The feast of the Presentation recalls the old man Simeon's song of thanksgiving for having lived to see the Messiah. His *Nunc Dimittis*—"Let thy servant depart in peace"—is part of the Church's evening prayers. In 542 in Constantinople, the emperor Justinian added it to the Eastern liturgy.

This year the feast fell on Super Bowl Sunday. Human nature instinctively finds entertainment more compelling than edification, but like all things ephemeral, games pass away while the songs of saints will endure until the end of time. Few today remember the Isthmian games of the Greeks, or the cheers in the Roman circus. But those games also warn thinking people of the dangers in giving sports a cultic status. When the amateur is overwhelmed by professionals who are paid mind-boggling salaries, inflating the cost of tickets, and whose lives and deaths distract from the great events of the day, a culture's perspective becomes irrational.

Add to this the *ad verecundiam* fallacy, by which people accept the unqualified opinions of individuals simply because of their celebrity. This applies to sports figures and Hollywood starlets who turn entertainment into political theater.

[1] This essay was adapted for *Crisis* from the author's weekly parish newsletter.

Our Peculiar Times

The aforementioned Justinian had to deal with this problem. He and his empress Theodora were not the only couple to have rooted for opposite teams; however, their situation was serious, since the teams represented political and religious factions. Theodora was a fan of the Greens, who were Monophysite heretics, and the emperor supported the Blues, who were orthodox Chalcedonians. No one who collects abstruse sports statistics should object that these theological issues are too obscure. Feelings were so intense in 532 that the Nika riots (*nika* being the term for "victory," now adapted for Nike sneakers, made mostly in third-world countries under disputed labor conditions) led to the deaths of thirty thousand rioters and the destruction of much of the city.

Super Bowl halftime extravaganzas surpass in their vulgarity only the Field of the Cloth of Gold games in France in 1520 when Henry VIII, twenty-eight years old and an impressive 6'1", wrestled Francis I, twenty-five years old and over 6'5". Thousands of tents were erected for the crowds, and for refreshments there were three thousand sheep, eight hundred calves, three hundred oxen, and fountains flowing with wine. Even the Ottoman sultan Suleiman I donated for entertainment dancing monkeys painted gold.

During the reign of Antiochus IV Epiphanes (175–164 BC), the Greeks built a gymnasium at the base of the Temple Mount in Jerusalem. Even some Jewish priests of the Herodian temple succumbed to the sports mania. Should any pulpit orator have tried to beguile his congregation on the feast of the Presentation with banter about the Super Bowl, let him be reminded: "Despising the sanctuary and neglecting the sacrifices, [the priests] hastened to take part in the unlawful proceedings in the wrestling arena after the call to the discus" (2 Macc. 4:14).

February 4, 2020

Pollyanna among the Prophets

Gerbert of Aurillac and Bi Sheng of Hubei were roughly contemporary (946–1003 and 990–1051), but Europe and China are far from each other. It is a pity that these men could not meet, for it would have been a unique match of minds. Gerbert became the first French pope—as Sylvester II—with an intelligence "off the charts" by any standard, and certainly so as an inventor. He introduced Hindu-Arabic numerals to the West, improved the celestial sphere, and invented the pendulum clock and what we would now recognize as a pipe organ. By constructing the first digital counting device as well as an abacus that mimicked the algorithm used today for arithmetical computations, he has claim to being the father of the modern computer, centuries before Pascal. During the Song dynasty, several decades after the death of Sylvester, Bi Sheng developed a moveable albeit cumbersome type, due to its porcelain blocks.

Johannes Gutenberg seems to have developed his own printing apparatus by 1440, and there followed a slow improvement to the rotary press in 1843 and offset printing in 1875. Gutenberg's invention opened the way for propaganda in the best and worst senses. Gutenberg spent his last impecunious years in the court of Archbishop Adolph of Nassau and was buried as a Franciscan tertiary, but his invention was eventually appropriated for spreading the new Protestant apologetic. Along with Martin Luther, pamphleteers such as Urbanus Rhegius and Philipp Melanchthon made adroit use of the printing press to describe in lurid detail the low moral state of Rome. The appeal of the vernacular was particularly effective, since Catholic apologists such as Hieronymus Emser and John Eck were mainly defensive.

These several centuries later, "social media" has changed culture in ways that even the brilliance of Sylvester II and Bi Sheng could not have imagined, and the invention of the Internet has multiplied incalculably the impact of Gutenberg's mechanical innovation. As with the sixteenth-century pamphleteers, the present reality and potential future test the virtue of prudence. Sometimes aggressive journalism tells the truth in ways that embarrass defensive apologists. The idle mind might wonder whether Charles Borromeo or Francis de Sales would have used blogs, but the prolific correspondence of these saints more closely resembles tweeting, their intellectual and literary superiority notwithstanding. Later, the saints Anthony Mary Claret in Cuba and Maximilian Kolbe in Japan would study printing and become exemplars of effective Catholic journalism.

This simply is a reminder that the scandals, vulgarities, and inarticulate thought that bombard social media may falsely give the impression that the present confusion in the Church is unprecedented. It may be singular in some ways, but it is certainly not without antecedent disgraces. It is fortunate that in the days of the Papal States, for instance, investigative journalists were rare. This is not to excuse the current state of affairs, but there might have been similar—or perhaps even worse—temptations to despair had earlier ages had access to the Internet.

There is a false and ephemeral piety that would deal with bad news by pretending it does not exist, or by censoring it when it cannot be ignored. This would be the Pollyanna complex: "Oh, yes, the game was to just find something about everything to be glad about—no matter what 'twas." Pollyanna Whittier started out well as the fictitious young orphan heroine in the 1913 novel by Eleanor Porter. Pollyanna's gossamer optimism was not unlike that of Wodehouse's Madeline Bassett, who held the view that "the stars are God's daisy chain, that rabbits are gnomes in attendance on the Fairy Queen, and that every time a fairy blows its wee nose a baby is born." But the relentlessly cheerful debutante of positive thinking was so irritating that Pollyanna's name became a byword to less blissful souls, rather like Voltaire's Pangloss, a satire of Leibnitz skipping through "the best of all possible worlds."

Pollyanna lives on in a parallel ecclesiastical world of new springtimes, new evangelizations, second Pentecosts, conferences of "diocesan leaders" with mic'd up motivational speakers "celebrating the life and dignity of the human person," and Falstaffian clergymen bereft of sense and burdened with unction. Catholic writers who confuse innocence with naïveté may print anodyne words that in the storms of the day become fatal to fact. They are to theology what Barney the Dinosaur is to paleontology. Thomas Paine, that most effective pamphleteer (his *Common Sense* still holds the record as America's best-selling printed pamphlet), wrote of the "summer soldier and the sunshine patriot." Although he was no friend of religion, his disparaging words take on a deeper mordancy when applied to anyone who enlists in the Church Militant without putting on the armor.

In Pollyanna's illusory ecclesiastical bubble are the Rex Mottrams of the frequently cited *Brideshead Revisited* scene in which he declares that the pope can forecast the weather (today that would be "climate change"). Flattery is Pollyanna's protocol. There even was a clergyman in the service of the pope who said that the Church "is openly ruled by an individual rather than by the authority of Scripture alone or even its own dictates of tradition plus Scripture." Flattery is an etiquette that sustains the transparent bubble that is popped with dangerous ease by the cynic. Disraeli was a master of that: "Everyone likes flattery, and when you come to royalty you should lay it on with a trowel." Update that to the evangelist Billy Graham's comparing President Eisenhower's first foreign-policy speech to the Sermon on the Mount. And, of course, there was the ridiculous attempt of the Pharisees and Herodians to "trap" Christ through insincere praise (see Matt. 22:16).

Human respect sometimes makes objective criticism difficult. I once insisted that my Korean violin teacher abandon his politeness and criticize my mistakes, but the best he could manage was: "You are now holding the bow like Jascha Heifetz ... but you do not sound like Heifetz." In Ancient Greece, *parrhesia* was a rhetorical form of frank speech correcting "those to whom one owes reverence, because we feel justified in pointing out some fault." As a dialectical device, Plato would simply call it a kind of "speaking truth to power." Those secure in themselves should welcome it. It is said that in 1670 King Louis XIV appointed the court preacher Bossuet tutor to the Grand Dauphin precisely because he did not want his heir coddled by *flatteurs*. St. John Paul II—successor to St. Peter, who himself was simply a man (see Acts 10:26)—told the effusive biographer André Frossard, "You are more of a papalist than I am." And in a rougher diction, made more poignant in the light of later curial turpitude, Pope Francis spoke in 2013 of prelates who "have often been narcissists, flattered and thrilled by their courtiers." "The court," he said, "is the leprosy of the papacy." Whatever he meant by that, and this Holy Father can be opaque at times, there certainly is a manipulative instinct in the sycophantic types such as Dickens's Uriah Heep and Trollope's Obadiah Slope. And slick Iago used unction to ruin Othello. If humility is the ground of all the virtues, this pastiche of humility is their annihilation. "Faithful are the wounds of a friend; but the kisses of an enemy are deceitful" (Prov. 27:6, KJV).

Famous from their source in Japanese culture are the "Three Wise Monkeys" known as Mizaru (See no evil), Kikazaru (Hear no evil), and Iwazaru (Speak no evil). It is easy to make them models of human wisdom, as Gandhi did when he adapted them to Hindi and claimed them as his only possession: Bapu, Ketan, and Bandar. But they can also be the Evil One's mockery of wisdom as willful ignorance, like idols before whom fools bow in delicate groves (Ps. 135:15–18). When the Three Wise Men entered the court of King Herod, they did not do so as those blind, deaf, and mute monkeys. Though they were from "a foreign land" they were familiar with the prophets whose words in Sacred Writ they had pondered, and thus they easily saw through the king's coyness. By one count, the Old Testament has forty-nine prophets, and none of them thought that the stars are God's daisy chain and rabbits are gnomes. And there were seven prophetesses—Sarah, Miriam, Deborah, Hannah, Abigail, Huldah, and Esther—but none was named Pollyanna.

In her own day, Flannery O'Connor grew impatient with the "happy news" of church newspapers. In contrast today, there may be an overabundance of muckraking print media, but the same prudence that disdains it should not altogether ignore it. As was first said in the eighteenth century, in an issue of Addison and Steele's daily publication the *Spectator*, a broken clock is right twice a day.

We have the hard lesson learned from the Legionaries of Christ scandal. In 2007, Pope Benedict abolished its special vow of "charity," which had forbidden any criticism of the order's superiors. Its culture of impermeability was an esoteric camouflage for corruption. In recent months, the Holy See changed the name of its Secret

Archive to "Apostolic Archive," to avoid misunderstanding, and the practice of the "pontifical secret" has been lifted in cases of sex abuse.

In his *Historical Sketches*, St. John Henry Newman distinguished detraction from discernment and noted "that endemic perennial fidget which possesses certain historians about giving scandal." He continued, "Facts are omitted in great histories, or glosses are put upon memorable acts, because they are thought not edifying, whereas of all scandals such omissions, such glosses, are the greatest."

King David was prophetic; he was not Pollyannaish. As he approached Bahurim, a man named Shimei pelted the king with stones: "Begone, begone, you man of blood, you worthless fellow!" David restrained Abishai and his other officials from killing Shimei, saying, "Let him alone, and let him curse; for the LORD has bidden him. It may be that the LORD will look upon my affliction, and that the LORD will repay me with good for this cursing of me today" (2 Sam. 16:7, 12–13).

Prophets are not reeds shaken with the wind, nor do they glide whistling through history, inoculated by innocuousness. Rather, they are patient because the Master said, "Heaven and earth will pass away, but my words will not pass away" (Matt. 24:35). And Heaven and earth include cyberspace.

January 27, 2020

Fifty Years On

The year of 1969 was a time of the finest and the worst, when most institutions, equipped with the polished trophies of new science, seemed to be having a mental breakdown. A man walked on the moon. But there were riots, protests, and a moral fragmentation whose detritus now controls the seminal arbiters of culture. The tone of thought at the heart of it was a composite of bewilderment, fascination, and obtuseness.

I have rarely written about the days when I was formed into a particular way of ordering my thinking, with a reluctance born of an intuition that looking back might make me brittle as a pillar of salt or soft as sentiment, for nostalgia can be a lethal alchemy. The sound and scene from fifty years past do not need to come alive again, for they never faded in my recollection. It seems like yesterday that I sat in a chapel of the ambulatory of the cavernous Cathedral of St. John the Divine in New York. I signed an oath of conformity to the Thirty-Nine Articles with a quill pen from a silver inkstand and then processed behind a verger with a heavy mace to the sanctuary of the largest Gothic cathedral in the world, as it proudly called itself. For on the twentieth day of December in 1969, unaware that twelve years later I would become a Catholic priest in another cathedral in the same city a short distance away, I was ordained an Anglican priest in a ceremony grand in itself but still small in the perspective of the important events of that year.

The processional hymn for the ceremony was "I Bind unto Myself Today." While the original is attributed to the Lorica of St. Patrick, the translation sung was by Mrs. Cecil Frances Alexander, wife of the Anglican archbishop of Armagh. We had been imbued with the assurance that Patrick himself would have been an Anglican if given the opportunity, and this confidence was expressed by the bishop whose sarcophagus our procession passed: once, when asked if there was salvation outside the Episcopal Church, the Rt. Rev. William Manning answered: "Perhaps so, but no gentleman would care to avail himself of it."

A canon sonorously read from the great pulpit the proclamation of intent to ordain: "We, Horace William Baden Donegan, Bishop of New York, Commander of the British Empire, Doctor of Divinity, et cetera, et cetera ..." The hard "c" in Oxbridge pronunciation distinguished the Latin of the Caesars from that of the popes. Years later, I learned that Bishop Donegan, always kind to me and never failing in graciousness, had been born in England of an Italian father named Donegani and had changed his name. When he died at ninety-one, his obituary said that his hobbies included listening to Gilbert and Sullivan operettas and playing golf while spending summers in London at the Ritz. My first interview with him before I entered seminary consisted in a conversation about the Queen Mother, to whom he would later, at Clarence House, present me, and all the while a Corgi she had given him sat on my lap.

My seminary days at the General Theological Seminary in New York City were vibrant with the Oxford Movement, and life in that close was a time machine with no intrusion from the passing century. Erudite and patient tutors, often august moral paragons, taught verities older than the fashions of the day. If a creeping violence against classical reason was infesting the world outside, there was little sense of it within those walls. We took seriously the confidence of the seventeenth-century bishop of Ely, Simon Patrick, for whom Anglicanism represented "that virtuous mediocrity which our Church observes between the meretricious gaudiness of the Church of Rome and the squalid sluttery of fanatic conventicles." Or rather (as that Aristotelian golden mean was sometimes put in more strident ways), ill distinguishing ascetics from aesthetics, we were satisfied to have a privileged perch somewhere between the painted harlot on the hills of Rome and the slovenliness of the Evangelical wench in the valley.

The bell that rang the time for Evensong was also the signal for sherry before we went into the chapel in our academic gowns. Fr. Louis Bouyer was of the opinion that the Daily Office, as arranged in the Book of Common Prayer and sung to Anglican chant, provided "a means of education by worship of which no Church, Catholic or Protestant, has the equivalent today." There is a certain wistfulness in that assessment, given that Bouyer and the Benedictine liturgist Bernard Botte quickly and under duress cobbled together the Eucharistic Prayer II of the Novus Ordo—supposedly channeling St. Hippolytus—at a trattoria in Trastevere. But in our High Victorian chapel in Chelsea Square, all was redolent of John Betjeman's reverie of "Anglo-Catholic Congresses": "The bells and banners—those were the waking days / When Faith was taught and fanned to a golden blaze." And how can I forget the good men who tutored me in veneration of Scripture and holy song? They come to me now like ghosts, not ghastly as of Endor, but as good men who tethered themselves to a meandering heritage that glanced away from its flaws—and a propensity for hanging and quartering of saints—to acknowledge Christ as Lord of history and agent of virtue. There was enough space in that contented world to accommodate Anthony Trollope and P. G. Wodehouse along with the venerable divines Lancelot Andrewes and Thomas Ken.

Our Peculiar Times

Has all that gone? Demographics make clear that where it once flourished there will be nothing left of Anglicanism after this remnant generation. How it happened so suddenly was a surprise only to the preoccupied. An Anglican bishop of Chinese birth who escaped the Maoist revolution told me that during an overnight stay he learned that his entire chancery staff were clandestine Marxists. Even so, in any cultural revolution, there are bureaucrats smiling harmlessly while planning harmful New Dawns in a pantomime of Pentecost.

A valiant attempt by Pope Benedict XVI to preserve some of that ethos has taken shape in the Anglican ordinariate, but it had a frail start. In the United States, many if not most of those involved were not reared in that tradition, nor have they been able to explain precisely what constitutes the ethos they want to preserve. For my part, I cannot think myself worthy of the gentle and selfless men and women—many formed in the better ways of an Edwardian haze—who eased the difficult rites of passage to maturity.

I am not aware that anyone from my day in the cathedral fifty years ago remains alive. Our Creator in His generosity made all things, but He neglected to give me perfect pitch as part of His bounty, as those who hear me chant at the altar readily know, but all those blessed and splendid souls I knew are providing some sort of descant—prescinding from the judgment of the holy Doctors of the Church as to where they may be. The missionaries who took the gospel to the ends of Empire, when the unsetting sun was high in the sky, wove part of the spiritual fabric I inherited, and in their name we fervently sang, in the trebles of choirboys, "From Greenland's icy mountains to India's coral strands ... " Having since embraced the fullness of what was preached back then, I know that the babies I first baptized had cries no different from those I pour water on now, and the bond that binds those on sickbeds—both long ago and now—is a strong one.

When I published my first book, warning that the Episcopal Church was embarking on a Gnostic course that, if altering the maleness of Holy Orders, would lead to an inversion of Holy Matrimony and a nightmare of eugenics, I was charged by many who said they once had hopes for me, with extravagance of statement and even disreputable fanaticism. It is no consolation now to know that I was right.

I am made anxious by the foreboding fact that there are those who, thinking themselves Catholic, would endorse the gross moral and doctrinal mistakes that have brought about the collapse of Anglicanism, which, quivering in its last throes, is sustained only by prudently invested endowments. The collapse of the old tradition was predictable, having been founded on the venality of a rapacious king, but the foundation of the True Church on the Rock of Peter is not a guarantee that winds will not whistle through empty convents and shrines in America and Europe, just as arid winds now blow over the vacant ancient dioceses of North Africa.

Let mine be a letter of affection without reproach, from one whose roots disdain emotion, to those who were patient with me when I first took up the promise to serve God, albeit in a mix of innocence and naïveté. There was a blessing and benison in my ignorance of the many trials that would lie ahead, for had I "loved to choose and see my path," I would have hesitated. One cannot pretend that the path to Rome was more difficult than what one frequently found upon arrival. If there are more years allowed me in the course ahead, I may write a lengthier story of my experiences, though in some quarters it might be a precipitate of agitation. Suffice it to say that St. John Henry Newman was an agent in my conversion. Once, standing in his pulpit in the University Church of St. Mary the Virgin, I felt something like a bolt of lightning. At the moment, I did not understand it. Now I do. Newman said that as a Protestant "I felt my religion dreary, but not my life — but as a Catholic, my life dreary, not my religion." Lacking his depth of soul, I never knew dreariness in any quarter. But if wistfulness is a pastiche of agony, I at least have known that no human journey is without interruptions of happiness.

Only after many years did I go back to my old seminary where my modest achievements were not without laurels. I went with hesitation and only at the bidding of a classmate who was visiting. It was hard to recognize the front building, and I was told by an officious clerk to apply by a side gate. Having rung the bell, a voice on an intercom told me to return the following Monday. Stranger still was the day I went, after many years, to the huge Cathedral of St. John the Divine to pay respects the day before his funeral to Horace William Baden Donegan of many honors, et cetera, et cetera. His coffin reposed in the "bare ruin'd choirs, where late the sweet birds sang." I was alone save for one silent clergyman in a tweed jacket and a nun moving her lips in prayer.

There is no sadness in all this, for days are too short for the indulgence of reverie and too full of the graces Our Lord never ceases to send. I have only gratitude for the exalted moments and for those occasional depths that are nothing other than harbingers of rising again. There are lessons to be learned in everything for an alert mind, and the ardent lesson I have learned is that there is the Word that never passes away, and any words in substitution for that Word witness to the unchanging God by their own changing.

> *Round the decay*
> *Of that colossal Wreck, boundless and bare*
> *The lone and level sands stretch far away.*

December 20, 2019

Our Patient and Indulgent Mother Church

A few decades ago, I had lunch with Daniel Carroll in Howard County, Maryland, during which he used a pop-up toaster in his grand dining room, which was hung with ancestral portraits. There were many such portraits, for Dan was a direct descendant of the only Catholic signer of the Declaration of Independence, Charles Carroll of Carrollton. Doughoregan Manor has been a private residence since it was built in the early eighteenth century, although its family chapel was open to area Catholics in days when the Faith had been proscribed. After the Civil War, the chairs in the chapel, where the signer is buried, were purchased by a maternal antecedent during a trip to Paris when the Church of the Madeleine was being renovated. I never got to go back to Doughoregan, but Dan wrote to say that he was using the incense I had given him.

What matters here are those chairs, for they were used at the funeral of Chopin. The "Raphael of the piano," as Heinrich Heine called him, had requested that Mozart's *Requiem* be played at his obsequies; special permission was granted for female singers, who were concealed behind a black velvet curtain, which must have posed an acoustical challenge. Pauline Viardot, who had affectionately nursed Chopin in his last illness, sang the mezzo-soprano part of the "Tuba mirum" movement. The soprano, Jenny Lind, had recently returned from America, where P. T. Barnum had paid her an unheard-of $150,000; she had vain hopes of returning to New York with Chopin. One of the pallbearers was the Romantic painter Eugène Delacroix, long rumored to have been the natural son of the diplomat and sometime bishop Talleyrand. Three thousand devotees packed the great Neoclassical church. For all the black crepe, Chopin's funeral was a colorful Catholic moment.

In the peccadillos, inconsistencies, and paradoxes of celebrities such as Chopin is displayed the mixture of sublimity and earthiness that constitutes the moral texture of Catholicism: an elasticity of accommodation that unsubtle critics confuse with hypocrisy, and a generosity of spirit that zealots (both secular and religious) scorn as indifference. Chopin is but one of many witnesses from his own age to the patience that Catholicism has for the creative mind, and even what the Romantic Age named "genius." Such patience is at risk today when sentimentality indulges a false mercy, not knowing the difference between steadfastness and rigidity, and confusedly loving the sin as part and parcel of loving the sinner. The Church, rather, is like the Scriptures as described by Pope Gregory the Great in his commentary of Job: a river broad and deep, shallow enough here for the lamb to go wading, but deep enough there for the elephant to swim—"planus et altus, in quo et agnus ambulet et elephas natet."

That expansiveness expresses the solicitude of Holy Mother Church in nurturing souls. Her patience and indulgence are infinite, but humans are not, so her benefaction requires contrition, the lack of which is the sin of presumption compounding all particular sins.

Chopin was born in Poland to a French father and a devout Polish mother. Chopin's Catholicism was unquestioned but fragile when faced with the social volatility of France, where he immigrated in 1831. Not even worldly Warsaw had prepared Chopin for the louche allurements of Paris, and his string of dalliances are part of musical lore. The demanding polonaises Chopin wrote while living in France seem to sublimate elegantly his frustrations as an exile who was undeniably comfortable with the new kind of domestication offered by the swooning *salonistes*. Amantine Lucile Aurore Dudevant (known to us as George Sand) was, of course, the most famous of Chopin's devotees; though the full nature of their relationship remains unclear, it could not have been what Plato proposed in the *Symposium*. She considered herself a Christian, albeit with an ephemeral, Romantic Christology that did little for Chopin's theology.

Dying in his apartment at 12 Place Vendôme in Paris circa 1849 at the age of 39, probably from complications of tuberculosis, Chopin politely resisted the pleas of his friend and fellow émigré, the Polish priest Aleksander Jełowicki. Various biographies give the same account: "In order not to offend my mother," Chopin told Jełowicki, "I would not die without the sacraments, but for my part I do not regard them in the sense that you desire. I understand the blessing of the confession in so far as it is unburdening of a heavy heart into a friendly hand, but not as a sacrament. I am ready to confess to you if you wish it, because I love you, not because I hold it necessary."

The priest persisted throughout Chopin's last four days, during which Protestant friends joined Catholics praying at the bedside.

At last, Chopin professed his faith in Christ, and received the sacraments with devotion, asking those present in the room to pray for him. He told Fr. Jełowicki, "My friend, without you I would have died like a pig." He called out the names of Jesus, Mary, and Joseph as he clutched a crucifix, saying: "At last I have reached the source of my blessedness."

Death came for Chopin on October 17 at 2:00 a.m. In accordance with his wishes, Chopin's eldest sister Ludwika Jędrzejewicz secreted his heart in a jar of cognac back to Warsaw, where it was buried in the Church of the Holy Cross. Chopin's heart became so potent a symbol of the Polish national spirit that it was stolen by the Nazis, who kept it until the end of World War II. During the bloodshed of the war, Chopin's legacy remained a source of solace and strength for the Polish people. One month after the Nazi invasion of Poland in September 1939, Pope Pius XII comforted the besieged Poles by invoking the genius of "the immortal Chopin," saying: "If the art of man could achieve so much, how much more skillful must be the art of God in assuaging the grief of your souls?"

Chopin's contemporary Franz Liszt was another Catholic prodigy often unsuccessful in taming his appetites. There was a bit of give and take between the two composers, expressed on one occasion when Liszt added a few frills as a display of *sprezzatura*, or studied carelessness, to a Chopin piece. Chopin told him to stick to the score. At one point they had their eyes on the same woman, but Liszt was able to fend well enough for himself. By his mistress, the countess Marie d'Agoult, he fathered Blandine, Daniel, and Cosima, the future second wife of Wagner. By this time Liszt was a sort of mega rock star, giving much of his stupendous earnings to philanthropies, including the restoration of Cologne Cathedral and the Church of St. Leopold in Vienna. Rather like the Irish singer Bono, Liszt performed benefit concerts after natural disasters, such as the great flood of Pest, and the fire that destroyed much of Hamburg.

Although Gregory XVI condemned the political philosophy of Lamennais, the French priest saved Liszt from becoming a diehard rationalist. Liszt was not unique in finding no inconsistency in being both a Catholic and Freemason. He had an antecedent in Mozart. According to the newspaper of the Italian Episcopal Conference, *L'Avvenire*, and also quoted in the *Katholische Presseagentur Österreich*, in an interview at a music conference in Chieti in 2006, Cardinal Schönborn of Austria curiously denied that Mozart had been a practicing member of the Lodge: "There's no foundation for his frequently mentioned membership in the Masons." In Vaticanese, this "does not conform to the truth." Indeed, Mozart's last work was the *Little Masonic Cantata*. Truths are true, and facts are stern tutors. Later, a spokesman for the cardinal explained that he had been misunderstood, and meant to distinguish eighteenth-century Freemasonry from later forms.

In 1860, Liszt was all set to marry the Polish princess Carolyne zu Sayn-Wittgenstein, but the Russian tsar prevailed upon Pope Pius IX not to annul the princess's 1836 marriage to a Russian prince and military officer. Instead of marrying, Liszt became a Third Order Franciscan, taking Minor Orders as a porter, lector, exorcist, and acolyte. He was punctilious in his assigned duties. At Castel Gandolfo, the Vatican, and in his own rooms, he spent many pleasant hours with the pope, who called him "my dear Palestrina." Liszt set about to reform the desultory condition of music in the churches, promoting Gregorian chant and polyphony, and he took some theological studies in 1868 with Don Antonio Solfanelli. When he did perform, it always was in clerical dress, and Pius IX addressed him as Abbé.

There were those who accused Liszt of having sold his soul to the Devil, because his skill seemed preternatural in such works as the *Dante* Sonata and the *Mephisto Waltzes*. And he could, for instance, sight-read the score of Mendelssohn's Violin Concerto with his left hand while holding a cigar in his right. The same was said of Paganini's skill with the violin. Actually, Paganini could play three octaves across four strings, because he very probably had the long bones and flexible joints typical of Marfan syndrome. Abraham Lincoln had the same.

Although Lincoln played no instruments, he learned to love opera, having seen his first in New York City two weeks before his inauguration: the American premiere of Verdi's *Masked Ball*, with its violent assassination scene. During his presidency, Lincoln attended the opera thirty times and saw his favorite, Gounod's *Faust*, four times. The Lincoln boys, Willie and Tad, were required to take music lessons on a new Schomacker piano in the White House's Red Room, with Polish instructor (and Chopin devotee) Aleksander Wołowski. As an aside, Rachmaninoff almost certainly had Marfan syndrome, and there are those who think that is why he and few others could play as written the opening chords of his Piano Concerto no. 2 in C. At his final recital in 1943, Rachmaninoff played Chopin's funeral march.

As for Paganini, he was as flamboyant a showman as Liszt. He played up the rumors of diabolism by dressing in black and riding in a black coach pulled by four black horses. His gaunt appearance was heightened when he lost all his teeth by the age of forty-six in 1828 due, evidently, to what morphological tests have confirmed as mercury treatment for syphilis. His appeal to the ladies increased, nonetheless. In that same year Paganini separated from his mistress Antonia Bianchi, by whom he had a son named Achille. Though ill in 1840 in Nice, he refused the ministrations of a priest sent by the bishop, for he did not think he was dying, though he soon did. Not having received the Last Rites, and compromised by rumors of diabolism, his body was refused interment in consecrated ground. Four years later, Pope Gregory XVI gave permission for burial in Genoa, and in 1876 Paganini was grandly entombed in Parma.

On October 27, 1850, one month following Pope Pius IX's restoration of the hierarchy to England after three centuries, St. John Henry Newman used the occasion of the installation of Dr. Ullathorne as the first bishop of Birmingham in St. Chad's Church, the work of Pugin, to defend the patient and indulgent ways of Holy Mother Church toward her beclouded children. As an experiment, I calculated that his sermon "Christ upon the Waters" must have taken at least one hour and fifteen minutes to preach. He addressed the matter of scandals:

> There are crimes enough to be found in the members of all denominations: if there are passages in our history, the like of which do not occur in the annals of Wesleyanism or of Independency, or the other religions of the day, recollect that there have been no Anabaptist pontiffs, no Methodist kings, no Congregational monasteries, no Quaker populations.

One pedantic quibble: the great Newman was wrong about no Methodist kings. Five years earlier, the very year that Newman was received into the Church, the first Methodist king of Tonga was crowned. Tuʻi Kanokupolu Tāufaʻāhau had been converted by Wesleyan missionaries in 1831.

Tom Mozley, the husband of Newman's oldest sister Harriet, said that his brother-in-law had "attained such proficiency on the violin that had he not become a Doctor of the Church, he would have been a Paganini." Assuredly this was not a reference to Paganini's domestic arrangements.

Once in Paris at the tomb of Chopin in Père Lachaise Cemetery, I was approached by a woman veiled in black who asked me to place flowers on Chopin's tomb. That I did, climbing over a railing and scaling the rather high plinth to place the roses in the arms of a mourning Euterpe, muse of music, sculpted by Auguste Clésinger. I can say only that I once prayed for Chopin's soul and immediately I was able to play the *Revolutionary* Étude, op. 10, no. 12, with far fewer mistakes than usual. Now, at risk of presumption, I should ask Paganini to help with my fiddle.

November 5, 2019

How to Write Your Own Encyclical

The cracks in the Axis powers became clear when the Armistice of Cassibile was announced on September 8, 1943, after the Italian government broke with the Nazis and joined the Western Allies. The National Socialists under the codename *Unternehmen Alarich* tried to take over the Italian zones of occupation in southern France and the Balkans before disarming the army of Italy itself, but they were foiled. Like the people they led, Hitler and Mussolini were birds of very different feathers, and their marriage of convenience was bound to fail. As languages reveal the psychology of the people who speak them, German and Italian are almost drolly unalike. For instance, German has many words for "invade," such as *überfallen*, *einfallen*, and *einmarschieren*, while Italian for the most part simply has *invadere*, used more often than not in the passive voice.

What the German language may lack in mellifluousness (although *Lieder* have their beguilements) it makes up in its brilliant precision. If words are inadequate, it just makes up new ones by cobbling old ones together. While German may be superior for expressing thought, the elegant art of the Italian language lies in its ability to articulate vacuity. Or, more precisely, it employs melodic vowels to give the occasional impression of thought when there is none. Here, of course, the ghosts of Dante and Petrarch may stir to haunt me, but they were derivative of the Latin school. It is a long and downward spiral from Cicero to Il Duce.

This past summer, what is now called the John Paul II Pontifical Theological Institute for Marriage and Family Sciences was "reconstituted" with an abruptness and thoroughness that scandalized over forty international scholars, who objected to the firing of several distinguished professors. It was a real purge—a term for which German has many equivalents such as *Säuberung* and *Reinigung*, but which Italian invariably would call *epurazione*. The Institute retains the name "John Paul II," but that serves now only as an ironic reminder that it has distanced itself from the theology, philosophy, and prophetic vision of that pontiff.

Archbishop Vincenzo Paglia, president of the Vatican's Pontifical Council for the Family, oversaw the "reconstitution" of the Institute, of which he is also grand chancellor. When he was bishop of Terni-Narni-Amelia, Msgr. Paglia commissioned a large mural by Ricardo Cinalli, an Argentinian whose Uranian appetites are on full display in the erotic figures depicted—including the future grand chancellor. In 2016, Paglia also supervised the publication of a Vatican-approved sex-education booklet; in response, Dr. Richard Fitzgibbons, a psychiatrist who was a consultant to the Holy See's Congregation for the Clergy and adjunct professor at the John Paul II Institute for Studies on Marriage and Family at the Catholic University of America, said: "This obscene or pornographic approach abuses youth psychologically and spiritually."

In 2015, at the time of the Synod on the Family, Archbishop Paglia called for an end to "ecclesiastical gobbledygook" that "sterilizes families." Perhaps to avoid the kind of "foolish consistency" Ralph Waldo Emerson called the "hobgoblin of little minds, adored by little statesmen and philosophers and divines," the grand chancellor contradicted himself by appointing as president of the John Paul II Institute a cleric not guiltless of gobbledygook (*discorso senza senso*). This summer in his address at the opening of the new term, Msgr. Pierangelo Sequeri orated:

> The recomposition of the thought [*ricomposizione del pensiero*] and practice of faith with the global covenant [*l'alleanza globale dell'uomo*] of man and woman is now, with all evidence, a planetary theological space for the epochal remodelling of the Christian form [*un luogo teologico planetario per il rimodellamento epocale della forma Cristiana*]; and for the reconciliation of the human creature with the beauty of faith. To put it in the simplest terms, by overcoming every intellectualistic separation between theology and pastoral care, spirituality and life, knowledge and love, this evidence must be rendered convincing for all: the knowledge of faith cares about the men and women of our time.

When he was finished, no one asked him what he meant, although there may have been much between the lines that should not have been said. It sounded too enchanting to mean less than its affected portentousness.

Several decades ago, I was subjected to a ritual oral examination, a *vive voce* for a degree in the University of Oxford, before a tribunal of professors whose imposing presence in their academicals made the prospect of the Day of Judgment like a frolic. But they turned out to be quite kindly souls, if of different schools of thought on God and man. To my surprise, after they perused the hundred or so pages of my dissertation, their only criticism was that on an obscure page there was a line containing "academic jargon." It was an edifying, and obviously memorable, complaint, even though the don making it harbored a Christology that might not have passed a test administered by St. Athanasius. The point was: if you know what you are saying and believe it to be true, make it clear—and not just to dons, but to everyone.

That was a different time, a different place, and a different culture. And the dons wore their learning lightly.

Descent into jargon to give the impression that obscurity is profundity is a temptation indulged not only by ecclesiastics, for it luxuriates in the ivied halls of academia and the labyrinthine corridors of government. But it parades with colorful panache in the Church, and it can bewitch even in English translation. If you make a list of jargonish adjectives and another of jargonish nouns, you are on your way to writing your own neoplastic academic speech, papal address, apostolic exhortation, or even your own encyclical. Look through the ever-lengthening volumes of the *Acta Apostolicae Sedis* and other pontifical sources, and you can find inventive adjectives such as "integrally ecological," "planetary," "dialectical," "epochal," "nuanced," "ontological," "clericalist," "osteoporotic," "neo-Pelagian," "leprous," "sloth-diseased," "schizophrenic," "paradigmatic," "issue-oriented," "cosmetic," and "pickled pepper–faced." Then in the column of nouns you can list, for starters: "field hospital," "coprophagist," "nominalist," "soap bubble," "rigidity," "peripheries," "paradigm," "dicastery," and "ecological debt."

By switching back and forth, or by occult inspiration, you can construct prophetic-sounding platitudes such as: "integrally ecological field hospitals," "planetary coprophagists," "dialectical nominalists," "epochal soap bubbles," "nuanced rigidities," "ontological peripheries," "clericalist paradigms," and "pickled pepper–faced ecological debts." Then you can start crisscrossing: "issue-oriented coprophagists," "paradigmatic consequentialists," "sloth-diseased nominalists," and so forth. You can even describe "planetary field hospitals," "osteoporotic nominalists," "epochal peripheries," and "schizophrenic clericalists." It's fun, and might have been the sort of pastime the late imperial senators in moth-eaten togas engaged in while the Ostrogoths menaced the crumbling Roman walls in the sixth century. Mathematically there are hundreds and indeed thousands of possibilities, and enough verbiage to keep paradigmatic dicasteries busy forever, *per sempre.* Or, to be more precise: *Jargon wird niemals kaputt sein.*

September 23, 2019

A Grammar of Dissent

Analytical psychology provided a virtually limitless opportunity for Carl Jung to play with the canonical vocabulary, expanding it to describe what he thought to be wider realms of human consciousness. An example of his creativity was his concept of *synchronizität*. This "synchronicity" described what he perceived to be "meaningful coincidences," by which he meant events that seem to have some sort of significant relationship even though they lack any apparent causal relationship. The more he considered this, the more he expanded his definitions.

Dr. Jung didn't go beyond the limits of his own science to claim that God is involved in these phenomena, but others have. G. K. Chesterton called coincidences "spiritual puns." There is a common instinct to attribute convenient phrases to Einstein, so it is not certain that he really did say, as is often claimed, that coincidences are God's way of remaining anonymous. But many thinkers—an overplus of them Frenchmen, such as Anatole France and Théophile Gautier—have said almost the same thing.

Since I wrote a book on coincidences (which, with a lack of imagination, I called *Coincidentally*), I was neither surprised, nor did I fall to my knees, when I was informed that on the very same day that I published my most recent essay for *Crisis* on the Vatican's use and misuse of adjectives, our Holy Father condemned the use of adjectives outright.

In an audience held in the Sala Regia of the Vatican Apostolic Palace and granted to the employees of the Dicastery for Communication and the participants in the plenary assembly of the dicastery, Pope Francis said:

> We have fallen into the culture of adjectives and adverbs, and we have forgotten the strength of nouns. The communicator must make people understand the weight of the reality of nouns that reflect the reality of people. And this is a mission of communication: to communicate with reality, without sweetening with adjectives or adverbs.

Whether this coincidence between the pope and me has any significance, I cannot say. In fact, my views on adjectives were somewhat different from the Holy Father's. There was no conscious collusion. Indeed, the pontiff often makes opaque allusions whose meaning can be interpreted variously, and whose full portent may belong to that vast corpus of thoughts whose true sense will be revealed only on a day known to God alone (cf. Luke 2:35). Not even his chief admirers claim that Pope Francis is a prodigy of pellucidity.

But he was clear about one thing, and he said so: he is "slightly allergic" to the use of adjectival and adverbial words such as "authentic and authentically," and "true and truly," as qualifiers of the word "Christian." The mission of communication, he said, "is to communicate with reality, without sweetening with adjectives or adverbs." He warned that "this culture of the adjective has entered the Church."

The Holy Father's heartfelt desire to persuade all Christians to rejoice in that sturdy title "Christian" without the need of qualifying adjectives such as "authentic" (although the word "Christian" is both an adjective and a noun) has an apostolic integrity in the best light. However, there is nothing absolutely wrong with adjectives. After all, "Catholic" can be a helpful adjective, and so can "Holy." There is no report of how this description of a grammatical invasion by adjectives was received by the listeners in the audience, but the ears of aesthetes might have prickled when the Holy Father went on to identify adjectives (and presumably adverbs) with rococo art. In fact, in an aside, he declared that rococo art is not beautiful. Besides being a personal judgment, which the pope himself has cautioned against, it must have been unexpected by those listening at quarter to nine in the morning.

Obviously, if inexplicably, this is a subject that animates the pope to a certain intensity of feeling, and he did not shy away from casting Watteau, Fragonard, Canaletto, Guardi, Belotto, Tiepolo, and Piranesi into disrepute—probably along with the proleptic grotesques of Raphael in the Vatican Loggia. Before the five hundred communicators, Pope Francis proceeded to compare rococo art to "strawberries on the cake!" The exclamation point used in the official transcript conveys a sense of his ardor.

This was not the first time he used this metaphor. On December 5, 2014, in an address to the Congregation for the Doctrine of the Faith, he provoked complaints from a few female theologians when he called them "strawberries on the cake."

Pope Francis used yet another gustatory metaphor. To emphasize the need for Christian communicators to give all of themselves without reservation for the propagation of the gospel, he invoked an Argentinian expression: "He puts all the meat on the grill." This harmless and even quaint phrase unfortunately—and perhaps also by some Jungian synchronicity—was uttered on the same day the United Nations' summit on anthropogenic climate change called for a decrease in meat consumption.

Our Peculiar Times

This theory about the weather, which the pope himself strongly accepts, has become for many an apocalyptic cult whose creed brooks no contradiction. Even adolescent girls are induced to weep in public at the prospect of climate-change cynics stealing from them their "dreams and childhood." One of them, who gave a histrionic speech at the United Nations, has Asperger's syndrome; thus, putting her on display might well be called child exploitation. Apropos a carnivorous culture, while Argentina exports 51 million head of cattle each year (its cattle produce 30 percent of its greenhouse-gas emissions), that country's National Institute of Agricultural Technology has tried to be ecologically responsible by developing a system by which digestive gases from bovine stomach cavities are channeled through a tube into a tank. Since a single cow emits upwards of 300 liters of pure methane daily, this can provide enough energy to keep a refrigerator working for 24 hours.

Although the Holy Father has not visited his homeland since becoming pope, this is something of which he might be aware and approve. He even addressed the crisis of methane gas in *Laudato Si'* (nos. 23–24). The opportunities herein for conservation are boundless. Much social benefit would accrue if that Argentinian invention could somehow be applied to celebrities, academics, politicians, and prelates.

The Holy Father certainly would not intend his attack on adjectives such as "authentic" to be read as an absolute. He himself has, from time to time, lapsed into its use. Before he was pope, on April 20, 2000, he published the prayer "On Authentic Priesthood." He has spoken of "authentic pastors" (January 26, 2018) and "authentic Christians" (April 25, 2018). He has described "authentic conversion" (January 26, 2018) and spoken of "authentic conversions" (August 21, 2019) as well as "the authentic basis of human life" (November 28, 2018). On the forty-eighth World Communications Day, he called for "an authentic culture of encounter" (June

1, 2014); the January 9 before that, he commended "authentic faith." In his Angelus address as recently as August 12, 2019, he said: "We are invited to live an authentic and mature faith."

During his address on September 23, Pope Francis quoted his patron: "Preach the Gospel, if necessary, also with words." But St. Francis of Assisi never actually said that. This attribution is as uncertain as the quotation above about God's using coincidence to remain anonymous. The venerable Dr. Martin Routh, an Oxford classics scholar and president of Magdalene College, summed up the wisdom of his life's experience as he approached his hundredth year in 1854: "You will find it a very good practice always to verify your references, sir!" There is, though, verity in Chapter XVII of St. Francis's Rule of 1221: "No brother should preach contrary to the form and regulations of the holy Church nor unless he has been permitted by his minister.... All the Friars ... should preach by their deeds."

This certainly was the message Pope Francis was trying to get across. If the way he said it was somewhat befuddling, that could only be due to his propensity to toss away his script and speak "heart to heart." In fact, he mentioned "heart" four times in the course of his remarks, beginning:

> I have a speech to read.... It's not that long; it's seven pages ... but I'm sure that after the first one the majority of you will fall sleep, and I won't be able to communicate.... I will allow myself to speak a little spontaneously, with you, to say what I have in my heart about communication. At least I think there won't be many who will fall asleep, and we can communicate better!

That must have caused amusement in the audience, but perhaps less so among any sensitive members of the Dicastery for Communication who had written the seven pages. For it is a well-known and even necessary practice for busy men to have ghostwriters. Matthew, Mark, Luke, and John had the Holy Ghost.

An obligation attaches to the grammar that speaks heart to heart, however, and that duty consists in a simultaneous use of the brain. Sentiment detached from thought will lead down wayward paths. This "heart-to-heart" language — the *cor ad cor* of St. Francis de Sales, which St. John Henry Newman made his motto — is always clear. Newman described the process of attaining certitude in his *Grammar of Assent*. Few minds could match his, just as few could equal his word-craft, and no one could be confused about what he thought or how he said it.

That is not a mere coincidence. It's thankworthy that Pope Francis will canonize Newman. Let it be a reminder to all that, no matter how nouns and adjectives and adverbs are employed, messy thinking is a Grammar of Dissent.

September 30, 2019

Pontifical Chic

In 2013, Pope Francis sonorously and rightly enjoined the bishops of the world: "Avoid the scandal of being 'airport bishops'!" An almost obsessive compulsion of some prelates to travel beyond their own dioceses evokes the absenteeism of the Middle Ages, when many bishops and abbots were seldom seen among their own people. The pope travels with astonishing frequency — surely with no little toll on himself, considering the burdens of age — but this might be justified to some degree by the fact that he is the universal pastor, with worldwide and immediate jurisdiction, according to canon law.

Nonetheless, the precedent set by his recent predecessors can impose a sense of obligation to travel, as if a pope is remiss if he isn't constantly on airplanes. Most pontiffs were effective, and perhaps more affective, when staying in Rome. Given arguments in favor of globetrotting, there is a danger that universality might be confused with internationalism. Considering the daunting cost-liness of such journeys, the plaintive apostrophe of Noël Coward obtains: "Why do the wrong people travel, travel, travel / When the right people stay back home?"

There is also the peril of overexposure. A pope now is even expected to give freewheeling chats while on airplanes, and this has led to off-the-cuff remarks that the Holy Father's communica-tions staff subsequently redact into a benign and coherent form.

Our Peculiar Times

Jochen Hinkelbein, president of the German Society of Aerospace Medicine, has warned that the air pressure on a jet airplane can match that atop an 8,000-foot-tall mountain. This can cause hypoxia, reducing the oxygen in blood by up to 25 percent; this is particularly harmful to the elderly and those with breathing difficulties. Pope Francis is an octogenarian and has only one lung. Without careful monitoring, say experts, this can affect the ability to think and speak clearly.

Pope Francis has nevertheless braved the challenge in a desire to reach his far-flung flock. In 2015, upon arrival in Bolivia, that nation's culture minister announced that the Holy Father requested coca leaves to chew. Although coca was declared illegal after the 1961 U.N. Convention on Narcotic Drugs, Bolivia withdrew from the convention system, maintaining a domestic coca market, and so the leaf is available there to mitigate altitude sickness.

This month, Pope Francis encouraged many people in Mozambique who desperately need moral support: their country, which was officially socialist until 1990 and still is not an electoral democracy, ranks 184th out of 187 countries on the U.N. Development Programme's Human Development Index. In the Zimpeto sports stadium, the pontiff said boldly: "Mozambique is a land of abundant natural and cultural riches, yet paradoxically, great numbers of its people live below the poverty line. And at times it seems that those who approach with the alleged desire to help have other interests. Sadly, this happens with brothers and sisters of the same land, who let themselves be corrupted."

It was a message that needed to be heard not only by that nation's political leaders, but also by some theorists in the Vatican itself who have gone so far as to extol China and other oppressive regimes as ethical paragons, while disparaging the United States—a country almost unique in the disaster aid and developmental assistance it has been providing Mozambique. On the other hand, China has been exploiting that country through oblique loan debt. Perhaps it was not coincidental that just before the papal visit to Africa, the Jesuit journal *America* featured an article entitled "The Catholic Case for Communism." It asserted:

> In fact, although the Catholic Church officially teaches that private property is a natural right, this teaching also comes with the proviso that private property is always subordinate to the common good. So subordinate, says Pope Francis in a truly radical moment in *Laudato Si'*, that "the Christian tradition has never recognized the right to private property as absolute or inviolable, and has stressed the social purpose of all forms of private property."

The pope's witness in Mozambique was somewhat compromised by those who, perhaps with the best intentions, vested the pope in a chasuble decorated with leopard skin orphreys. Perhaps Roman advisors thought this would signal some sort of empathy with the indigenous culture. If so, they were mistaken. It was an echo of that low point in 2000 when liturgists at the third-millennium celebrations in St. Peter's Basilica provided hired men dressed as Africans in leopard skins, blowing trumpets made of elephant tusks, oblivious to regulators of the ivory trade. The leopard design worn by the pope in Africa must have been synthetic because, as the liturgical designers apparently did not know, there are practically no leopards in Mozambique. Indeed, in 2018, a leopard was seen in Gorongosa National Park for the first time in fourteen years. At least one German cardinal with Teutonic superiority, Überlegenheitskomplex, still refers to Africa as "the Dark Continent."

Our Peculiar Times

Affecting leopard haberdashery may have been witless stereotyping, but it does resemble the patronizing sort of "radical chic" that Tom Wolfe satirized in his 1970 essay describing a cocktail party Leonard Bernstein hosted in his Park Avenue duplex for leaders of the Black Panthers, when he served watermelon hors d'oeuvres.

Scottish drummers still wear leopard aprons. This dates back to the nineteenth century, when the Scots included Africans, who were the best drummers, in their regimental bands. These days, the skins they wear are faux. In 1970, Pope Paul VI (at whose canonization traditional vestment–makers were not conspicuous) abolished cardinalitial ermine and the bearskin helmets of the Corps of Gendarmerie. Even Britain tried to replace the bearskins of the Grenadier Guards—a privilege granted after Waterloo, beginning with the First Regiment of Foot Guards—and other units, but found that the fur from culled Canadian black bears was much better in every way. If the pontifical liturgists wanted to be "woke," as the neologism has it, instead of leopards they should have imitated the skins of real Mozambique wildlife: impala, nyala, and kudu.

For those who really want to keep up with these curiosities, the only African religion that uses leopard skins as ritual vesture (along with monkey tails) is *Shembe*, a relatively new amalgam of Christian and Zulu customs in South Africa's KwaZulu-Natal region. Even that cult seems to have felt the long arm of PETA, and one of their leaders, Lizwi Ncwane, recently announced: "For the past (several) months now, we have been using fake skins because we are trying to bring awareness among our people."

Rather ominously, Pope Francis not long ago was pictured wearing a circlet of parrot feathers in preparation for the special pan-Amazon synod of bishops. Regrettably, he was not the first modern pontiff to do something like that, and it was more unsettling than the spectacle of Calvin Coolidge's donning a Sioux headdress upon his induction into the noble tribe in 1927.

The synod's *instrumentum laboris* includes a rhapsodic elegy to Stone Age culture beyond the reveries of Rousseau, while neglecting to mention the local practices of child sacrifice, cannibalism, and chronic intertribal belligerence: "Their diverse spiritualities and beliefs motivate them to live in communion with the soil, water, trees, animals, and with day and night. Wise elders … promote the harmony of people among themselves and with the cosmos." Alas, the Catamari mission among the Yanomami people has not had a single conversion in fifty-three years. Radical chic cannot change this.

Self-conscious attempts to flatter a people can be as demeaning as bigoted subjugation. If the Church is truly universal, she need not try to mottle what is Militant, Expectant, and Triumphant in her supernatural charisms by lowering herself to mere syncretistic internationalism. One can only hope that, at the canonization of John Henry Newman, the pope does not carry a cricket bat.

In an exclusive 2018 interview with Vatican News, the official news service of the Vatican's Dicastery for Communication, former vice president Al Gore said that Pope Francis "has been at the forefront in leading the world toward constructive climate action" and that he was "grateful for and in awe of the clarity of the moral force [the pope] embodies." But Mr. Gore is not flawless in his impressions, nor is he exact in his exegesis. In contradistinction to the prophet who said that a leopard cannot change its spots (Jer. 13:23), the *Toronto Sun* quoted the radical-chic Gore on November 19 as saying, "We all know the leopard can't change his stripes."

September 13, 2019

Infandum: 18 Years On[2]

In 1789 George Washington prayed in St. Paul's Church, on what we now call lower Broadway, on the day of his inauguration as the first president of the United States. The churchyard was already old. On September 11, 2001, several new corpses were lying on the old graves. A temporary morgue was quickly set up in a nearby hotel. All that the Founding Fathers stood for was contradicted in a thunderous attack on the heart of the city that calls itself the capital of the world.

Grown children had grown accustomed to taking prosperity for granted and had often scorned the virtues that created the prosperity. The frenzied celebrations of the third millennium were largely conspicuous for their cheerful banality. There were fireworks but no great blazing works of art. A generation after men went to the moon, celebrants did circles on Ferris wheels; in London a dome was built with no particular purpose in mind and was hastily filled with just about everything except an altar to God. The general euphoria was tinged with melancholy, almost like that of Alexander with no more worlds to conquer. What to do with endless peace? Some said that history had ended. Then came an airplane flying so

[2] This essay was first published under the title "*Infandum*" in the November 2001 print edition of *Crisis*.

low, in a city that usually does not notice noise of any kind, that I had to take notice.

Crowds screamed and ran when the first tower fell; when the second came down, many just sat stupefied on the ground and groaned. Those buildings were not widely loved by New Yorkers. In the 1960s when Penn Station was dismantled, they were built with the rebarbative euphoria of the "International School," whose architects and sycophantic political backers defied everything that had gone before. An architect famously complained that the towers "tilted" the Manhattan skyline.

They stood, nonetheless, tall evangels of great enterprise, and at night when their cold steel was a shadow and their lights flooded the harbor, they could stun sullen eyes. Those who saw them collapse felt a collapse in themselves. About 25 percent of the onlookers are said to have experienced post-traumatic stress, a syndrome that can be traced back to the silence of our first ancestors as they left Eden in shock. Helpless reporters, kept at a distance, heard from eyewitnesses responses like that of Aeneas when Dido asked him to recount the loss of his ships and sailors: "Infandum, regina, iubes renovare dolorem." (Oh Queen, you bid me retell a tale that should not be uttered.)

The horrific shock treatment of September 11 has rattled three modern assumptions. The first was the politicized dismissal of natural law. George Washington in his pew at St. Paul's believed in the inalienable right to life. The primacy of natural law was vindicated when people at the World Trade Center struggled to rescue one another, often sacrificing their lives to do so. A man leaving his apartment to go to work in one of the towers heard his wife crying that she was going into labor. Instead of going to his office, he took her to the hospital and watched his baby enter the world as his building collapsed. The baby's first act was to save his father. In a world of carnage in Bethlehem, men once heard the cry of the baby who saves all those who call upon Him, through all ages, even as late as September 11, 2001. The thousands of lives crushed on that day will make it harder to say that life doesn't count.

Secondly, the holy priesthood has been a victim of modern assault. God's gift of priestly intercession had recently become an object of incomprehension and mockery. Books were written on how the priesthood might be reformed out of existence. A saint once said that a priest is a man who would die to be one. On September 11, a chaplain of the New York City fire department, Fr. Mychal Judge, was crushed by debris while giving the Last Rites to a dying fireman. Members of his company carried Fr. Judge to New York's oldest Catholic church a few blocks away and laid him on the marble pavement in front of the altar. Each knelt at the altar rail before going back to the flames. I stayed a while and saw the blood flow down the altar steps. Above the altar was a painting of Christ bleeding on the Cross — the gift of a Spanish king and old enough for St. Elizabeth Ann Seton to have prayed before it. More than local Catholic history was encompassed in that scene. For those who had forgotten, the Eucharist is a sacrifice of blood, and it is the priest who offers the sacrifice. September 11 gave an indulgent world, and even delicate catechists, an icon of the priesthood.

The fall of the towers quaked modern man's third error: his contempt for objective truth. The whole world said that what happened on September 11 was hideously wrong, and suddenly we realized how rarely in recent times we have heard things that are hideous and wrong *called* hideous and wrong. So many firemen wanted to confess before entering the chaos that we priests gave general absolution. They would not have wanted to confess if they didn't know the portent of the moment; nor would they have made the sign of the cross if they thought existence was a jumbled quilt of inconsequential opinions. A rescue worker next to me boasted that his lucky penny and his little crucifix had saved him when he was tossed ten feet in the air by the reverberations of falling steel. He got up, brushed himself off, and went back into the bedlam. If he was superstitious, he was only half so. The Holy Father has often been patronized by savants who thought that his description of a "culture of death" was extravagantly romantic pessimism. They have not spoken like that since September 11.

A crowd of people blinded by smoke were panicking in a Wall Street subway exit. One man calmly led them to safety. He was blind, and he and his guide dog knew every corner of that station. One might say—and if one were rational, one would have to say—that each generation, culturally blinded in ways peculiar to its age, is offered a hand to safety by people whose holiness is often considered a handicap. At the World Trade Center, rescued men and women were heard to use words such as "guardian angel" and "savior." Days later, confession lines were long and congregations stood in the streets outside packed churches. One waits to see if grace will build upon grace.

Perhaps it would be naïve to hope that a new Christian consciousness suddenly and smoothly will arise. On a train a few days after the attack, I sat next to a teenager wearing the ritual garb of his atomistic tribe, backward baseball cap and such. When I recounted how rescuers had kept rushing into 240,000 tons of collapsing ironwork without any apparent thought for themselves, he replied in a voice coached by the sentinels of self-absorption: "They must be sick." It will take more than one September day to humanize a generation.

We were attacked on what was to have been the day of the primary elections for the city's mayoral office. One policeman, speaking through a gas mask, gasped how all this chaos made all those candidates and all their "issues" seem so small. (That is only the gist of what he said; he used sturdy monosyllabic Tudor metaphors appropriate to the passion of the moment.) I do not see that problem being quickly cured. Bill Clinton, still unaccustomed to his reduced place in life, arrived on the scene the day before the president. The spectacle of his pumping up oceans of empathy in front of cameras carried bad taste to a length he had not managed even in the White House. Sobered by the day's events, the media virtually ignored him. As a chronicler said of Napoleon, "He embarrassed God." Within days, an organist from another state faxed offers of special fees to parishes whose organists could not manage the number of funerals. A company from Maine advertised handheld devices that send sonic vibrations to soothe grief.

Such inanities of the human race can be understood only as little burps from Beelzebub's inferior minions. Beelzebub did not win the day against courage. In a World War II speech, Churchill paraphrased St. Thomas Aquinas in describing courage as the foundational quality for all the virtues. The politicians of his day who wanted compromise with evil do not share a place on his plinth, and nations that were neutral then do not boast of it now. When asked about evacuating Elizabeth and Margaret Rose during the Blitz, Queen Elizabeth famously said that the princesses "will not leave unless I leave, and I will not leave unless the King leaves, and the King will not leave." On September 11, through the roaring and crashing and screaming, it may be that many began to hear Christ the King as if for the first time: "I am with you always until the end of the world."

September 11, 2019

Nothing New under the Sun:
St. Bernard's Advice to a Pope

From a natural perspective, the difference that God makes is evident in whether human existence is cyclical or linear. Some eminent classical philosophers made sense of human experience only as repetitious, and that view migrated from Plato up to moderns such as Spengler and Santayana. The cyclical theory subjects human will to fate, but, as the Scriptures begin in an earthly garden and end in a heavenly city, life is not repetitive but progressive. That's why providence conquers fatalism.

The cyclical view is different from the sort of ennui expressed even in Scripture. "There is nothing new under the sun," we're told in Ecclesiastes. There's a hint of world-weary resignation, too, in Shakespeare's "Seven Ages of Man," chronicling how human nature never changes. That canticle to the aging process in *As You Like It* is by the same author who wrote: "What's past is prologue." Generations pass, but human nature perdures, and the spiritual DNA in Adam is endemic to every child of man: a nature fallen, but originally upright, and raised up again by the Resurrection of Christ.

Sometimes, the mind experiences what the vernacular philosopher Yogi Berra called "déjà vu all over again." It seems we've been there before.

Our Peculiar Times

Some neurologists call this "split perception" or "cryptomnesia." Seemingly forgotten information (which has, in fact, been stored deeper in the brain) is recovered in a dual neurological processing. At least, that's one physical explanation for why things unfamiliar suddenly seem familiar.

Morally, experience plainly brings to mind the fact that "history repeats itself"—not like a broken record, but in a progressive way, in which personality types and circumstances are "typical" regardless of changes in centuries and customs. This is why we can speak of "personality types," and why so many of the Church Fathers relished typology in their exegesis of the Scriptures—possibly, on occasion, even to the point of guileless excess.

If there is "nothing new under the sun" in terms of human nature, new people are nevertheless responsible for their actions. "New occasions teach new duties," as the hymn says, but it is possible to learn from how other people once handled similar situations.

One can take as an example the twelfth century, which is often looked upon as the dawn of a Golden Age of civilization. Yet its challenges prevent any assumption that our problems today are unprecedented. In the life of St. Bernard of Clairvaux (1090–1153), there are striking similarities between the centuries numbered twelve and twenty-one.

The accomplishments of St. Bernard—his travels, writings, and influence on culture in general—are exhausting just to read. The intensified Rule he instituted inspired the foundation of 163 monasteries of the Cistercian reform, from France to Germany, Sweden, Italy, Portugal, England, and Ireland. The fact that he accomplished all this in just 63 years, before modern travel and medicine, burdened with migraine, gastritis, hypertension, and anemia, testifies to the power of what he called the three fundamental virtues: humility,

humility, and humility. He never yearned for early retirement, nor would he have been a golfer.

As human nature never changes, the best and worst of Bernard's times foreshadow the same types now. The rising of great Gothic churches and the spread of universities were contemporary with schisms and corruption. Because of humility, humility, humility, Bernard dispensed with the kind of calculated diffidence that is humility's caricature, and he did not shy from exposing corruption. This annoyed Cardinal Harmeric, who thought Bernard was disrespectful to Pope Honorius II. "It is not fitting that noisy and troublesome frogs should come out of their marshes to trouble the Holy See and the cardinals," he sneered in a letter to the holy abbot. But even that complainer came around to admit the truth of what Bernard was writing from the *Val d'Absinthe* (Valley of Wormwood), which he happily renamed the Bright Valley, *Claire Vallée*—Clairvaux.

When one of his former monks, Bernardo Pignatelli, became Pope Eugenius III, Bernard undertook a series of writings, *De Consideratione*, on how to get it right. These were occasional pieces and not one fixed volume, as Cardinal Baronius mistakenly thought later on. They treat religious and secular authority, finances, law (Gratian's *Decretals* had finally put canon law into some sort of order), and scholarship when pedants were going off track by engaging in useless dialecticism, giving Scholasticism a bad name. "God is found more easily in prayer rather than in discussion," he noted.

Above all, the mystical quality of the Church must take precedence over (while not contradicting) her juridical aspect. Law is a friend of justice, but legalism becomes its enemy. "Perstrepunt in palatio leges, sed Justiniani, non Domini," Bernard complained to Eugenius. (Daily the laws resound in the palace, but they are the laws of Justinian, not of the Lord.) With poignant honesty,

Bernard also analyzed the miserable failure of the Second Crusade, which he had preached.

In Bernard's thirteenth letter to Pope Innocent II—the third legitimate pope before Eugenius, and whose cause he had championed against the claims of antipopes Anacletus and Victor—he sets the tone for how he will advise Eugenius: "To his most loving father and lord, Innocent, by the grace of God supreme pontiff, the devotion, for what it is worth, of Bernard called Abbot of Clairvaux. Scandals are necessary, necessary (Matt. 18:7) but unpleasant!" Later, he writes to his protégé:

> True, you sit on Peter's seat. What of that? Though you walk on the wings of the wind, you will never outstrip my affection. Love knows no lord . . . it is not so with some, not so: but they are moved with fear or avarice. These are they who seem to bless, but there is evil in their hearts; they flatter to one's face, but in the time of need they desert us. But charity never faileth.

A couple of generations after Bernard, the French cardinal Jacques de Vitry indulged a bit of stereotyping to describe students in the University of Paris. The English (he said) were drunkards, the French effeminate, the Germans obscene, the Burgundians vulgar and stupid, the Sicilians tyrannical and cruel, and the Romans "seditious, turbulent, and slanderous."

Bernard also surveyed types through a Gallican eye, but with a Galilean heart consumed by zeal for his Father's house. "Show me a man in the whole city of Rome," he wrote to Eugenius,

> who welcomed you as Pope without having his price, or hoping to get it. Even when they profess to be your very humble servants, they aim at being your masters. They pledge their

fidelity only that they may more conveniently injure the confiding. Hence it is that there can be no deliberation from which they think they ought to be excluded; there will be no secret into which they do not worm their way. If the doorkeeper keeps one of them waiting a minute or two, I should not like to be in his shoes. Now for a few illustrations, so that you may know whether I understand this people's ways, and how far. First of all, they are wise to do evil, but they know not how to do good. Hateful to heaven and earth, they have laid hands on both; they are impious towards God, heedless in holy things; turbulent among themselves, jealous of their neighbors, barbarous to foreigners, they love no man and are loved of none; and when they aim at being feared by all, all must fear. These are they who cannot bear to be beneath, though they are not qualified to be at the head, faithless to superiors, insufferable to inferiors. They have no modesty in asking, and no shame in refusing. They worry you to get what they want; they cannot rest till they get it; they have no gratitude once they have got it. They have taught their tongue to speak great things, when there is but little doing. They are lavish promisers, niggardly performers; the smoothest of flatterers, and the worst of backbiters; artless dissemblers, and malignant traitors.

His practical counsel to Eugenius in Book II of the *Consideration* includes a reminder that his lips are for sacred speech and should not engage "idle talk" and "buffoonery." What the pontiff says should be measured, infrequent, and solemn. In Book III, he moves on to the serious problem of avarice: "a vice from which your character is safe enough," but which tempts others. There were the problematic Germans with "moneybags" and others who used base bribes to gain favor and secure bishoprics. Here again the local curial culture was not impervious to mercenary allurements: "Was Rome ever known to refuse gold?"

In Chapter IV, Book II, Bernard glides to new heights of suffused indignation, and he enjoins discipline while not being naïve about changing behavior. "Is there anything in history more notorious than the wantonness and pride of the Romans?" he asks, calling them

> a race unaccustomed to peace, familiar with tumult; a race to this very day fierce and intractable; who will never submit except when they have no power to resist. Here is the mischief; this is the care that lies heavy upon you, and you must not disguise the fact. You perhaps smile as you read this, for you are convinced that they will never be cured. Do not despair: what is required of you is the care, not the cure.

The pope must be aware of, and not ignore, the dissolution around him, as it manifests itself in felinity and effeteness. He is directly responsible for his household, and laxity will only engender worse abuse. "Impunity is the mother of audacity, audacity brings forth excess," he warns. Thus in Book IV:

> In the look, dress, gait of the priests about your person you should allow no trace of immodesty or indecency. Let your fellow bishops learn from you not to have about them boys with their hair curled, or effeminate youths. It is surely unbecoming for a bishop to go hither and thither surrounded by fops who wear the turban and use the curling iron. And remember the admonition of the wise man, "They are thy daughters: make not thy face cheerful toward them."

This was not an uncommon problem in medieval courts, as the chronicles of St. Peter Damian attest. Bernard, who kept close correspondence with various countries, may have been aware that St. Anselm of Canterbury, while in Hastings with the royal court at the start of Lent, had refused to give ashes to epicene young noblemen who wore long curled hair.

In sum: times change, but human nature does not. The anapodoton *plus ça change* remains. And if some are enticed by the chimera of nostalgia to think that things were better in more tranquil ages than now, when profligacy is confederate with heresy, or to ask how was it possible for such good times to have collapsed so quickly, recall the 1953 encyclical of Pope Pius XII on St. Bernard:

> The Catholic faith, supreme solace of mankind, often languishes in souls, and in many regions and countries is even subjected to the bitterest public attacks. With the Christian religion either neglected or cruelly destroyed, morals, both public and private, clearly stray from the straight way, and, following the tortuous path of error, end miserably in vice.... Therefore, as the Doctor of Clairvaux sought and obtained from the Virgin Mother Mary help for the troubles of his times, let us all through the same great devotion and prayer so strive to move our divine Mother, that she will obtain from God timely relief from these grave evils which are either already upon us or may yet befall, and that she who is at once kind and most powerful, will, by the help of God, grant that the true, lasting, and fruitful peace of the Church may at last dawn on all nations and peoples. (*Doctor Mellifluus* nos. 32, 35)

August 27, 2019

Fr. Rutler's Guide to Virtue Signaling

Truths become truisms by being true. Shakespeare may have got some of his Aristotle through Ben Jonson; in any case, he has Polonius quoting the philosopher's truism about night following the day.

This is a roundabout way of saying that certain untutored impulses are inevitable, and one of them now is the annually predictable petition by "virtue signalers" in New York City demanding the removal of the statue of Theodore Roosevelt in front of the Museum of National History.[3]

That great museum is replete with engraved lines from his speeches, defiant of today's political correctness—for instance, his address to the Boy Scouts in 1912, praising the strenuous life and stressing the importance of self-defense comingled with chivalry. This was not bravado, but when morality is elastic, tenacity of purpose is suspect.

The fuss about the statue predates the recent iconoclastic hysteria that has pulled down statues across the land. To a purely aesthetic eye, few could match for quality that of Nathan Bedford Forrest in Memphis, which was removed notwithstanding the fact

[3] The museum, in a decision agreed to by the City of New York on June 20, 2020, announced that the statue will be removed.

that Forrest tried to disband the Ku Klux Klan (which he had led) because of its violence.

There remain over fifty buildings, parks, bridges, and monuments dedicated to Senator Robert Byrd, an Exalted Cyclops of the KKK who led the opposition to the Civil Rights Acts of 1964, which the Republicans were able to pass only through a final faltering of hostile Democrats. Virtue-signalers should cut Forrest the same slack they did for Byrd, but as virtue signaling is the display of moral superiority by asserting a virtue without having to practice it, it provides no harbor for logic.

Moral hauteur can be highly arbitrary. For example, it was morally invigorating for Yale University to erase the name of John Calhoun, who defended slavery, even though a committee headed by John F. Kennedy in 1957 ranked Calhoun as one of history's five greatest senators. But Yale keeps the name of its eponymous benefactor who made a fortune with the East India Company by trafficking in slaves. Virtue-signalers in the #MeToo movement should also deplore the way Elihu Yale abused his wife by keeping — not one, but two — mistresses.

There will always be contradictions if those of great accomplishment are expected to be flawless diamonds. To be consistent, the #MeToo movement should have something to say about the undisciplined priapism of the aforementioned John F. Kennedy and, if emboldened by honesty, Martin Luther King.

Nor should the virtue signalers in the Black Lives Matter movement give a free pass to the 77 percent of Democrats who voted against the Thirteenth Amendment in 1865, and who unanimously opposed both the Fourteenth Amendment overturning the Dred Scott decision, and the Fifteenth Amendment granting suffrage to black citizens.

Our academic institutions are glib when rationalizing the inconsistencies in their virtue signaling, as was Princeton University in its official explanation for why it would not remove memorials to Woodrow Wilson, who instituted Jim Crow in federal institutions and screened *The Birth of a Nation* in the White House. "It is important to weigh Wilson's racism, and how bad it was, with the contribution he made to the nation," administrators explained.

That generosity of spirit should also apply to the Theodore Roosevelt statue. As a work of art, it is a tour de force sculpted by James Earle Fraser and unveiled in 1940. His most famous works are the American Indian head on the "buffalo nickel" and the poignant figure of an exhausted Plains Indian, *End of the Trail*.

Fraser had grown up in Minnesota, familiar with the local tribes and enamored of their culture. This is evident in the figure of a generic Plains Indian in the Roosevelt group—the epitome of noble dignity—just like the African American figure, the third of the group, classically handsome and powerful. The platitudinous objection now is that Roosevelt is the only one on a horse, loftier than the others as one would expect to be in saddle, and thus, according to detractors, posing as superior in race and culture.

Isolated from the conditions of earlier generations, virtue signalers have difficulty appreciating those efforts of Roosevelt to make progress in racial matters. In 1901 he was the first president to invite an African American—his friend and advisor, Booker T. Washington—to dine in the White House. He was widely rebuked for doing so, most violently by those outside the Republican Party.

In 1929, when First Lady Lou Hoover invited to tea the wife of the only African American member of the House of Representatives—the Republican congressman Oscar de Priest—it occasioned a poem by a man in Missouri, which Senator Hiram Bingham of Connecticut called "vicious, obscene doggerel."

Roosevelt's handling of the Brownsville Affair in 1906 has been considered a low point in his race relations. He dishonorably discharged over a hundred black troops, but from a later remove, his insistence that his decision had been free of racial prejudice was not an exception to his characteristic honesty.

Living in the Dakota Badlands, and familiar with distorted tales of the American Indian Wars, Roosevelt had an unbecoming animus. "I don't go so far as to think that the only good Indians are dead Indians," he once said, "but I believe nine out of every ten are, and I shouldn't like to inquire too closely into the case of the tenth."

But that was when he was twenty-eight. By the time of his bombastic second inaugural parade in 1905, he had five tribal chiefs as marshals of honor, along with Geronimo, who was a leader of the Bedonkohe band of Apaches. Geronimo had made a career of shooting Mexicans in retaliation after they killed his mother, wife, and three children, and he extended his slaughter to unmitigated attacks on white people. He remained a prisoner of war held in custody at Fort Sill under benign conditions and was granted a temporary leave for the parade. His esteem for Roosevelt brought him to baptism in the president's Dutch Reformed Church, from which he was expelled four years later for gambling.

During Roosevelt's glory days in the Spanish-American War, his eclectic Rough Riders included Cherokees, Chickasaws, Choctaws, and Creeks. The charge up San Juan Hill was joined by two of the four "colored" Regular Army regiments, the Ninth and Tenth Cavalry, who were crucial to victory. But for the best of intentions, the president's policy of assimilation, based on the General Allotment Act (or Dawes Act) of 1887, to the extent of requiring that tribesmen get Western haircuts, was devastating for tribal culture.

Roosevelt was a child of his time like everyone else, but he was one of the rarer types who also changes the times. He never shook off his early *noblesse oblige*, but natural virtue shaped his development.

It is unlikely that these considerations mattered to the anonymous virtue signalers who defaced the Roosevelt statue at the museum two years ago under the cover of darkness. None would have qualified as Roosevelt's heroic "man in the arena," and he certainly would have disdained their use of fake blood. The inflated syntax of their press release said that their "counter-monumental gesture" was intended to do "symbolic damage to the values [the statue] represents: genocide, dispossession, displacement, enslavement, and state terror."

"Genocide" comes close to the one fault they overlooked in the man on the horse: eugenics. While Roosevelt thought that Darwin's confidence in the inevitability of human progress was absurd because it was based on biology rather than virtue, he did join the faddish eugenics movement.

The young Winston Churchill did the same. Churchill's mentor, the Irish American congressman William Bourke Cockran, took Winston to Albany in 1900 to meet then-Governor Roosevelt. No one had a greater influence on the formative Churchill than Cockran, whom he would quote in his 1946 "Iron Curtain" speech.

But the meeting was dismal, and Roosevelt told Henry Cabot Lodge: "He is not an attractive fellow." In words that Winston might have thrown back at him, Teddy objected to his "levity, lack of sobriety, lack of permanent principle, and an inordinate thirst for that cheap form of admiration which is given to notoriety." Among their differences, Roosevelt supported women's suffrage, which Churchill opposed. And he complained that Churchill did not rise when a lady entered a room.

Our Peculiar Times

As for moral inconsistency: in their selective obloquy, the virtue-signaling critics of the Roosevelt sculptural group did not object to Roosevelt's flirtation with eugenics, which he never completely repudiated. Similarly, Churchill, as First Lord of the Admiralty, attended the first International Eugenics Conference in 1912, along with Alexander Graham Bell, Charles Eliot of Harvard, and Sir William Osler, a founder of the Johns Hopkins Hospital and later Regius Professor of Medicine at Oxford. The conference's president was Charles Darwin's son, Major Leonard Darwin, who proposed "flying squads of scientists" to test for intelligence, in order to prevent the reproduction of the "feeble-minded."

For George Bernard Shaw, "The only fundamental and possible socialism is the socialization of the selective breed of man." Bertrand Russell would require "procreation tickets" for those who wanted children. In 1915, even the deaf and blind Helen Keller disconcertingly embraced eugenics, arguing against life-saving medical procedures on infants with severe handicaps on the grounds that their lives were worthless and they would likely become criminals.

Chesterton's pithy objections were ridiculed by the Anglican dean of St. Paul's Cathedral, William Inge, who called him an "irrational prophet." Opposition from the Catholic Church was dismissed as beneath consideration.

The term "eugenics," meaning "good genes," had been coined by Darwin's half-cousin, Sir Francis Galton. In fact, the criteria for superiority had more to do with social class than intelligence. While many, such as Churchill, demurred from sterilization, distinguished ranks did not: Sidney and Beatrice Webb, Harold Laski, and John Maynard Keynes were all pro. By 1927, Supreme Court Justice Oliver Wendell Holmes Jr. would famously opine on forced sterilization in *Buck v. Bell*: "Three generations of imbeciles are enough." In a vote of 8–1, the sole dissenter was Justice Pierce Butler, a Catholic.

Alexis Carrel often is extravagantly heralded as the model of a Catholic scientist because, having lapsed from the Faith in early years, in Lourdes he witnessed and acknowledged as miraculous the cures of a woman with tubercular peritonitis and of an eighteen-month-old blind boy. In the year of the first Eugenics Conference, he received the Nobel Prize in medicine for his work on vascular anastomosis.

However, he was not received formally back into the Church until 1942 by a Trappist monk, Alexis Presse. Meanwhile, he embraced eugenics and recommended gassing "undesirables." He invented the first perfusion pump in collaboration with Charles Lindbergh, a proponent of Nazi racialism. A collaborator with the Vichy regime and head of Pétain's "French Foundation for the Study of Human Problems," Carrel was placed under house arrest after World War II. Only Fr. Presse, who gave him the Last Rites as he died before standing trial, may have known if he recanted.

Then there was another Nobel laureate, Francis Crick, discoverer of DNA, who wrote after the war: "The main difficulty is that people have to start thinking [about] eugenics in a different way. The Nazis gave it a bad name and I think it is time something was done to make it respectable again." He died eighteen years after Margaret Sanger, whose bust in the Smithsonian Institution and statue in Boston's Old South Meeting House are unscathed, but lack her line: "A marriage license shall in itself give husband and wife only the right to a common household and not the right to parenthood."

Our Peculiar Times

These architects of the culture of death have memorials far and wide. Virtue-signalers who want real targets need not waste artificial blood on James Earle Fraser's statuary group. If they consider themselves beacons of virtue, they should first learn what virtue is.

August 8, 2019

An Immodest Proposal

A fad for picturesque ruins grew luxuriantly in the Romantic Revival from the end of the eighteenth century to about the mid-nineteenth, and where there were no real ruins, "follies" re-created them. Real ruins remain in a kaleidoscope of times and climes: Machu Picchu in Peru, Ayutthaya in Thailand, Stonehenge in England, Luxor in Egypt, and Baalbek in Lebanon. Some were simply left unfinished out of fear of curses, as with the Ta Keo temple in Cambodia, and the Mingun Pahtodawgyi (which would have been a five-hundred-foot-tall pagoda) in present-day Myanmar. Work on the Hassan Tower in Morocco, begun in 1195, stopped at the death of the caliph Yaqub al-Mansur.

Rather more prosaically, the National Monument of Scotland came to be called "Scotland's Shame" in the nineteenth century because money ran out. Bara Kaman, the mausoleum of Ali Adil Shah II, was left unfinished to prevent it from overshadowing Gol Gumbaz, the mausoleum of the sultan of Bijapur. Tourists ogle the walls of Pompeii submerged by a volcano. A young Oxonian won the Newdigate Prize for his poem about Petra in Jordan: the "rose-red city half as old as time." It decayed only because it had been abandoned, but nearly a million tourists go there each year now.

That young poet, John William Burgon, wrote those lines in the same year that Newman became a Catholic. They were parodied in doggerel about port, invoking Newman's geriatric tutor Thomas Short: "That rose-red liquor, half as old as Short." But as ruins go, if not one stone is left upon another, even in Jerusalem, their very existence cries out in ways that men do not, or even will not.

By a providence that nervous chroniclers call "luck," the fire in Paris did not ruin the Cathedral of Notre Dame. Most of its major parts remain, however fragile at the moment. Even the south rose window glows as the gift of St. Louis IX, who commissioned it in 1260. Its eighty-four images, or "medallions," are a mathematical canticle to eternity.

St. Louis's great-grandfather, Louis VII, provided one of the great scenes of medieval romance when he laid the cornerstone in 1163 along with Pope Alexander III. The king had supported the pope during a papal schism, and both were men of high energy and expansive vision. The pope devoted himself to strengthening the churches in Finland, Hungary, Portugal, Scotland, and Ireland. Likewise, King Louis VII consolidated his own duchies, visited Hungary, and went on to the Holy Land, having nearly been killed by Turks outside Laodicea. That familiar name is a constant reminder of that Laodicean mediocrity, a spiritual affliction a thousand years before King Louis and Pope Alexander, and one that still haunts and harrows episcopates in our own day (Rev. 3:15–16).

A year after the pope and the king laid the cornerstone, they welcomed the exiled Thomas Becket. His former mentor and later persecutor, Henry II, had become king of England as well as duke of Normandy and Aquitaine and count of Anjou. Seven years after construction began on the cathedral, Becket would be martyred. Things were further complicated by the fact that Henry had married the first wife of Louis, the powerful Eleanor, eighteen years earlier, immediately upon the annulment of her marriage to Louis.

Pope Alexander quickly canonized Becket in 1173 and showed his magnanimity by forgiving Henry after his show of penance with a sorrow not altogether feigned, and creating him Lord of Ireland. The pope was acting upon the controversial bull *Laudabiliter* of his predecessor Adrian IV. But Henry also responded to an appeal for protection from the king of Leinster, Diarmait Mac Murchada, against the threats of High King Ruaidrí Ua Conchobair.

St. Malachy, archbishop of Armagh, had tried his best to revive the Faith after it had fallen into desuetude in the melancholy and chaotic centuries after Palladius and Patrick, the sacraments largely neglected or abandoned. He restored the Latin liturgy and chants where Gaelic had crept in, and required the blessing of marriages. Passing through France on return from his second trip to Rome in 1148, St. Malachy died in Clairvaux in the arms of St. Bernard, having told him that the Gaels were "Christian in name, in fact pagans."

Pope Alexander envisioned the Anglo-Norman invasion of Ireland as an evangelistic obligation, not only to the Irish but also to the Vikings of Dublin. Though king of England, the Plantagenet Henry II spoke only French as did most of his army. From then on in France, contesting claims to rule were fraught with extravagant gestures: in 1431, two years after Charles VII was crowned as king of France at Rheims with St. Joan of Arc in attendance (accompanied by Scottish bagpipes), Henry VI was crowned as king of France in Paris in Notre Dame at the age of ten. At age seven, he had been crowned king of England in Westminster Abbey, his short legs dangling from the throne that is still used.

The desecration of Notre Dame in 1548 by Huguenots was matched only by the enormities of the French Revolution. The turning tides of belief and unbelief have not affected a common sense that the cathedral is like the heart of the nation, in stark contrast to the frigidity of the Pantheon. While it has been a focus for saints, there are others whose attitude is more tentative, like that of Winston Churchill, who did not pretend to mysticism and explained that he supported his Church of England like a flying buttress: from without.

At the liberation of Paris in August of 1944, a very mixed throng of people instinctively marched to the cathedral for a chanting of the "Te Deum" led by Charles de Gaulle: a difficult man but a true Catholic. He banned Cardinal Emmanuel Suhard from attending, because that archbishop of Paris, though suspect by the Nazis, seemed in his accommodation of the Vichy government to have been too Laodicean for the general.

A British intelligence officer, Malcolm Muggeridge witnessed the scene when a gunshot rang from one of the arches. "The effect was fantastic. The huge congregation who had all been standing suddenly fell flat on their faces.... There was a single exception; one solitary figure, like a lonely giant. It was, of course, de Gaulle. Thenceforth, that was how I always saw him—towering and alone; the rest, prostrate."

The buttresses and walls of Notre Dame remain, though its roof is gone. Outrageous proposals for modernizing it have been put forth by "starchitects," some of whom are of the dystopian mentality that imposed upon Paris the cultural incubus of La Défense in the department of Hauts-de-Seine, the Centre Pompidou and, one dare say, the Louvre Pyramid. They bring to mind part of Hilaire Belloc's lapidary reverie in the solitude of the Sahara while gazing upon the ruins of Timgad:

> The Barbarian hopes—and that is the mark of him, that he can have his cake and eat it too. He will consume what civilization has slowly produced after generations of selection and effort, but he will not be at pains to replace such goods, nor indeed has he a comprehension of the virtue that has

brought them into being. Discipline seems to him irrational, on which account he is ever marvelling that civilization should have offended him with priests and soldiers. . . . In a word, the Barbarian is discoverable everywhere in this, that he cannot make: that he can befog and destroy but that he cannot sustain; and of every Barbarian in the decline or peril of every civilization exactly that has been true.

The French Senate has passed a bill requiring that the cathedral be restored to its "last known visual state." This will include replicating the spire of the thirty-year-old Eugène Viollet-le-Duc. If they stick to that commitment it will be a triumph. It was only by the fortune of circumstance that the cathedral was not destroyed by Renaissance and Baroque snobs who thought it was an eyesore. The style known as *opus Francigenum* became known as "Gothic" only in the 1530s, when Giorgio Vasari mocked it for falling short of classical symmetry.

But an instinct inseparable from a desire to soar and shine draws all sorts to what began in the twelfth century, when Abbé Suger tutored that young man who planned on an ecclesiastical vocation and was surprised to find himself titled Louis VII upon the death of his elder brother, Philippe. Queen Eleanor complained that he was "monkish."

That "new style" was so organic that the restorers Jean-Baptiste Lassus and Viollet-le-Duc, not without their detractors, could add their own touches—such as the transept flèche with its crocks and statues, and the capricious gargoyles or chimera, which were added between 1843 and 1864—all in the same spirit and free of pastiche.

To everyone's recollections of the cathedral, I can add my own, for in that cathedral I had one of two experiences of my life that affected me definitively. The other I shall leave for another time, but I pay more attention now than I did in the summer of 1967, when I entered the cathedral for the first time as a student.

I was still an Anglican, and unfamiliar with the protocols of lighting votive candles, so I imitated how others did it before the fourteenth-century statue of the Virgin of Paris. I was moved by more than a tourist's curiosity, and perhaps I sensed something other than the aesthetic of the statue's High Gothic contrapposto. Anyway, sixteen years later back in Paris, I was a Catholic in Holy Orders and was able to attend Easter Vespers, but had to stand by the west doors because of the crowd. A man, who I assumed was some sort of usher, approached me and led me near to the altar and gave me the one vacant chair, which was directly beneath the Virgin of Paris. For a second time, I lit a candle.

Since so many have offered unsolicited opinions about the future of the cathedral, I would make an immodest proposal. For various unrecorded reasons, the cathedral was never finished, for surely Suger and Louis and Alexander envisioned spires that would be the prototypes of Chartres and Cologne and scores of others. After 1250, the west towers were left as they are now.

Our Lord gave His counsel, with which even the Senate of France would agree: "For which of you, desiring to build a tower, does not first sit down and count the cost, whether he has enough to complete it?" (Luke 14:28). Two spires would probably cost much less than a ballistic missile. Those who would object to the cost are probably the intractable types whose citation of Scripture is confined unwittingly to the tragic apostle (see Matt. 26:9; John 12:5). Viollet-le-Duc actually did a sketch for such towers, even taking into account the subtle difference in their sizes, the north being slightly larger.

Predictably, there will be those who are so accustomed to the unfinished condition they prefer it that way. The sentiment reminds me of a woman at the Academy of Music in the 1970s when Eugene Ormandy received an ovation as he made his first appearance after hip-replacement surgery. She muttered to me: "He looked more poetic with his limp." Admittedly, in his *Projet de restauration* of 1843, Viollet-le-Duc decided against building the western spires because that "would be remarkable, but would no longer be Notre-Dame de Paris."

Yet that may have been the influence of the project's co-author, Lessus. Exactly twenty years later, Viollet-le-Duc wrote in the first volume of *Entretiens sur l'architecture*: "The work is not yet finished; the two towers should be terminated by two spires to complete and explain the carefully studied lines of the lower structure."

Well, one can indulge a little wishful thinking, and what is most important is the restoration of what was lost. But to realize what was meant to be in the first place would confirm the sacred words of the prophet at the time of the Second Temple:

> Who is left among you that saw this house in her first glory? and how do ye see it now? Is it not in your eyes in comparison of it as nothing?... The silver is mine, and the gold is mine, saith the LORD of hosts. The glory of this latter house shall be greater than of the former, saith the LORD of hosts: and in this place will I give peace. (Hag. 2:3, 8–9, KJV)

July 29, 2019

Bastille Day and Other Convenient Myths

Centenarians are not as rare as they used to be, and one can profit from their memories. In California, I spoke with a woman who had traveled there from Missouri in a covered wagon. I visited another woman in a retirement home who was the first to hear her English professor at Wellesley College, Katherine Lee Bates, read a poem she had written on her summer vacation in Colorado: "America the Beautiful." These good women were blessed with active minds, and their memories were acute. Because "God is in the details," what they considered commonplace was most revealing: The Missouri woman's caravan traveled mostly by night because the weather was cooler and they were less conspicuous to suspicious tribesmen. Professor Bates was somewhat tentative regarding the quality of her verse and, as she hesitatingly unfolded her manuscript, asked the opinion of her students.

While the adage obtains that those who do not know their history are condemned to repeat it, those who do not know their history can also be fooled. "Bastille Day" is the celebration of an inflated myth. Propagandists — and later romanticizers such as Alexandre Dumas with his *Man in the Iron Mask* and the amiably pathetic Dr. Manette of Charles Dickens — made the storming of the prison the first thrust of the liberators. The Bastille was far from a fetid torture chamber. It had a storied history. While at times it must not have been a congenial hospice, the number of prisoners dwindled under benign Louis XVI, making it the equivalent of an American "white collar" place of custody, with tapestries, paintings, a library, and at least one personal chef.

On July 14, 1789, there were only seven inmates, a couple of them mental patients. Ten days earlier, the Marquis de Sade, not a paragon of virtue, ran along the rampart of the prison shouting lies about inmates' being murdered. This was too much for the congenial warden, the Marquis de Launay, to handle, and so the aristocratic patron of sadism was remaindered to a lunatic asylum in Charenton, founded by the Catholic Brothers of Charity, who were pioneers in psychotherapy. The Marquis de Sade left behind his unfinished 1785 magnum opus, *The 120 Days of Sodom*, in the Bastille.

Yet the myth of the dank dungeon persists, and the key to the Bastille, weighing just over one pound, now hangs in Mount Vernon, the proud gift of the Marquis de Lafayette, sent in the summer of 1790 via Thomas Paine to New York where it was displayed as a relic at a presidential levee, and then through Philadelphia to Virginia. As for the Bastille, its remnant prisoners were an afterthought since the revolutionaries had pulled down its gates to get hold of 250 barrels of gunpowder. Indeed the confused inmates seemed reluctant to leave. The kindly, if dour, Marquis de Launay was dragged out and brutally stabbed, and then a butcher named Mathieu Jouve Jourdan sawed his head off. The prison was soon torn down, but bits and pieces are preserved as relics.

It takes a propagandist skilled in shamelessness to airbrush the Reign of Terror, but it has been done many times, not least of all by our own Thomas Jefferson. When the Cathedral of Notre Dame burned this year, there was much misinformation about its history. During the Revolution, it was ransacked by thousands of hysterics and had most of its treasures looted, which included the decapitation of twenty-eight statues of the kings of Judah along with statues on the other portals. The building was mockingly desecrated as a temple of Reason with a woman of ill virtue dancing as a goddess on a fabricated "mountain" replacing the altar. Relics, vestments, and furnishings were destroyed, and images of saints were replaced with busts of such benignities as Voltaire and Benjamin Franklin.

Part of the lead roof was pulled down to make bullets, and the consequent leakage hastened the weakening of the stone fabric. The sonorous bronze bells were smashed and melted to be cast as cannons. The whole edifice might have been destroyed had not Napoleon attempted some repairs in the whitewashing and Neoclassical-pastiche theatrical set for his coronation, a triumph of *nouveau riche* over *ancien régime*. Only the Gothic Revival, animated in part by Victor Hugo's story of Quasimodo, prevented the ravaged shrine from being totally demolished. "Quasimodo" is from the Introit for the First Sunday after Easter, a quotation of 1 Peter 2:2 . The deformed bell ringer, childlike in his ways, was a foundling left at the cathedral on that Sunday. The name may also have been a medieval term for a miscarriage.

It was perplexing, then, to read an essay in *Le Figaro* by the estimable philosopher Sir Roger Scruton at the time of the recent fire at the Cathedral of Notre Dame. At first he waxed well about that architectural wonder as seen through the eyes of an Englishman: "We have done to London what Le Corbusier wished to do to Paris, and what one of our architects, invited by President Pompidou, did to the Marais. We have replaced built form by childish bubbles of steel and glass. Our churches stand in concrete deserts, and it is hardly surprising if nobody visits them or enters them for a time of prayer."

But then, astonishingly for a knight of eternal verities, he said of the thousands of hysterics who brutally clawed at the cathedral during the Reign of Terror: "Nobody at the time could bring himself to lay desecrating hands on the cathedral, apart from a few ruffians who beheaded a saint or two, thinking them to be kings." This was tantamount to saying that the Taliban simply sprayed graffiti on a few large Buddhas in Afghanistan out of theological pique. Horace granted that even Homer nods off; however, insouciance about such a notorious clash of cultures, especially from a laureled spokesman of classical perception, is worse than nodding off and is more like falling into a coma.

Perhaps a sensibility hopeful about man's better self could not abide the very idea of desecrating the sacred so blatantly. But if one has experienced the modern age, there is no excuse for thinking of human depravity as a leitmotif. The desecration of Notre Dame of Paris was a coruscating and indelible display of man's cruelty to himself as a frustrated image of God. Yet it remains poignant that the most cynical thinkers have mourned the terrible fire. In promising to restore it, President Macron made a remark that suggested there might be an opportunity for innovative architects to modernize it. This was fortunate because, given the contrarian spirit that has always been the provocative art of the Gauls, the reaction was fast and hard: to rebuild it just as it had been. On the other hand, if Macron had demanded that the cathedral be restored in perfect detail, there might have been cries for replacing it with a duplicate of the Los Angeles cathedral.

There are many myths fabricated to illustrate truths or attempts at truth. Santayana said that "myth is expression, it is not prophecy." That is why myths are not reliable. If Julius Caesar said anything at all to Brutus in his last difficult moment, it was "Kai su, teknon" and not the quotation found in Shakespeare. Nero did not really fiddle while Rome burned because, to be pedantic, he had a cithara at a time when there were no fiddles. Lady Godiva, wife of Leofric, kept her clothes on. Washington was an honest man, but that does not mean we should believe Parson Weems about the cherry tree. John Adams attested that the Boston Massacre was not a massacre.

Paul Revere did not ride alone through the night shouting the words of Longfellow, and not all who died bravely in the Alamo wanted freedom for everyone, for they had slaves—unlike the Mexican abolitionists. Just days ago in New York, people paraded to commemorate the riot at a Christopher Street tavern in 1969 that became a symbol for the civil acceptance of sexual inversion, neglectful of the facts that it had been owned by the Genovese crime family with no liquor license, had catered to underage youths, had given policemen protection from a mob outside, and was sub-sequently a juice bar, bagel shop, Chinese restaurant, and shoe store, and had transferred its name to a bar nearby.

It is better to take the counsel and share the memories of people who know what they are talking about. There is a special power in such witness that needs no embellishment and gives no harbor to fantasy, for its enchanters are chroniclers and not fabulists. Take, for instance, the father of a man I knew who stopped a conversa-tion about the Gettysburg Address by saying, "I heard it. I was a boy but I still remember it, and the reason there was no applause is just that people didn't know what to do."

The gospel is good news and not fake news, because it is real and not malleable putty in the hands of theorists looking for a story to illustrate an idea. The story is real, and the challenge ever since has been to figure out not how to make it fit us, but how we in our mix of doldrums and ecstasy can fit into it. "That which was from the beginning, which we have heard, which we have seen with our eyes, which we have looked upon and touched with our hands, concerning the word of life" (1 John 1:1).

July 12, 2019

U.S. Bishops Approve the Pope's Capital Punishment Ban

Saeva indignatio. Few writers in the history of English letters could express "savage indignation" at human folly as did Jonathan Swift, who wrote those words for his own epitaph. Our times give ample opportunity to empathize with him, and that is never more so than when clerics get together in large numbers.

Bishops have many daunting responsibilities and, if they are reasonable, they are not fleet of foot to beat a path to synods and conferences and plenary sessions and other impositions on their august office. Their patience in such meetings is exemplary, and so lesser souls should be patient with them when they sometimes fail to match up to Athanasius or Borromeo.

At the U.S. bishops' general assembly that took place June 11–14, 2019, in Baltimore, there were many items to discuss, chief of which was a protocol on how to handle prurient offenders, which passed under the lumbering title "Directives for the Implementation of the Provisions of *Vos estis lux mundi* Concerning Bishops and their Equivalents." *Vos Estis Lux Mundi* is the papal *motu proprio* issued on May 9, 2019, which prescribed procedures for holding bishops and religious superiors accountable for handling cases of sex abuse. Working within the framework of the Church's hierarchical constitution, it retains bishops as their own regulators, while acknowledging that their failures in the past have cost the Church billions of dollars in fines and punitive damages.

This brought to mind the poet Juvenal—a match for Jonathan Swift when it comes to savage indignation—when he asked in his *Satires*: "Who will guard the guards?" Swift and Juvenal together at a conference of bishops would have provided lively commentary. So would Samuel Johnson, for that matter. Dr. Johnson loathed Swift, probably because they were so alike in their instinct for righteous irritation, expressed in colorful ways in part, perhaps, because Swift was aggravated by an equilibrium disorder called Ménière's disease while Johnson almost certainly had Tourette syndrome. Juvenal's apostrophe "Quis custodiet ipsos custodes?" concerned the problem of randy guards guarding sex offenders. He proposed replacing them with eunuchs, not a practical solution today even with the current trend of "sex reassignment surgery."

The *saeva indignatio* emerging from the Baltimore meeting, however, was not the response to the *Vos Estis* document. After all, that issue has been a muddle for a long while. Rather, a more astonishing matter, though little noted by the multitude, was the assembly's handling of the controversial issue of capital punishment. Indeed, the bishops were informed that they were not to discuss the doctrine itself, but were only to consider the translation of a papal revision of the *Catechism of the Catholic Church* on the matter, specifically paragraph 2267. In 1992, John Paul II had revised this section, problematically inserting a prudential opinion discouraging lethal executions. But he also allowed that "assuming that the guilty party's identity and responsibility have been fully determined, the traditional teaching of the Church does not exclude recourse to the death penalty, if this is the only possible way of effectively defending human lives against the unjust aggressor." Supposedly, the latest revision exalts mercy at the expense of justice, neglectful of what the newly elected John Paul II said in a general audience in 1978: "There is no love without justice." Until the present day's climate of disdain for doctrine, "mercy and truth are met together" (Ps. 85:10, KJV), but, in the new dialectic, mercy has devoured truth altogether.

While John Paul's revised text maintained the authentic teaching and the legitimacy of such punishment, the inclusion of a prudential opinion in a catechetical exposition of established doctrine opened the way for abuse, as this writer among others predicted. Now this has happened in a blatant way, and it is all the more confusing for its inarticulateness. Specifically, the new section calls capital punishment "inadmissible because it is an attack on the inviolability and dignity of the person." Not for the first time in recent years, this woolgathering has opened a real can of worms. "Inadmissible" is not a theological term, and use of it without explanation is contentious. As a legal term, "inadmissible" means that it is not relevant to the case. In other words, capital punishment is to be treated as no longer relevant to justice, thus dismissing the magisterial structures based on natural law and Scripture. The cavalier treatment of natural law and scriptural evidence makes prospects for maintaining all moral doctrine fragile and all moral praxis subjective.

Aware of the monumental dangers of this, a group of prelates published a "Declaration of the Truths Relating to Some of the Most Common Errors in the Life of the Church of Our Time,"[4] which included a relevant point:

> In accordance with Holy Scripture and the constant tradition of the ordinary and universal Magisterium, the Church

[4] Edward Pentin, "New 'Declaration of Truths' Affirms Key Church Teachings," *National Catholic Register*, June 10, 2019, https://www. ncregister.com/daily-news/new-declaration-of-truths-affirms-key-church-teachings.

did not err in teaching that the civil power may lawfully exercise capital punishment on malefactors where this is truly necessary to preserve the existence or just order of societies (see Gen. 9:6; John 19:11; Rom. 13:1-7; Innocent III, *Professio fidei Waldensibus praescripta; Roman Catechism of the Council of Trent*, p. III, 5, n. 4; Pius XII, *Address to Catholic jurists* on December 5, 1954). (no. 28)

There have even been bishops so impatient with the subtleties that make theology logical that they have turned two thousand years of Christianity upside down by announcing that the death penalty is absolutely immoral. This epistemological novocaine contradicts an advisory of Cardinal Ratzinger in 1992: "If a Catholic were to be at odds with the Holy Father on the application of capital punishment ... he would not for that reason be considered unworthy to present himself to receive Holy Communion."

One supposes that the use of the term "inadmissible," clumsy as it is, is an attempt to shy from being explicit and even heretical on the matter. The canon lawyer Edward Peters wrote that "declaring the [death penalty] as immoral *per se* puts one *at risk* of asserting something that many qualified scholars argue powerfully *is* opposed to infallible Church teaching, and possibly even to contradicting something divinely revealed. The real possibility of so offending the truth should, I think, trigger more respectful caution by those in positions of authority when speaking on these matters" (emphasis original).

When the proposed revision of the *Catechism*'s section on the death penalty was introduced at the Baltimore assembly, one perceptive bishop asked what "inadmissible" means. The bishop selected to present the text said that the proposed draft provided "a context and justification for the development of this teaching on the dignity of the human person, but also emphasizes the continuity of Catholic teaching on the topic." Here at work is George Orwell's doublethink, which mitigates cognitive dissonance by proposing two contradictory statements as mutually complementary. Thus, doublethink claims with a straight face that to declare the death penalty inadmissible is identical to the Church's uninterrupted Magisterium, which maintained that capital punishment is admissible and even sometimes necessary. In 2019 as in *1984*, anyone who can make dissonance mellifluous by using a condescending facility of expression is considered an intellectual beacon, even when his intelligence is merely above average where average is modest. And this is because, as Erasmus wrote in his *Adagia*, "in the land of the blind, the one-eyed man is king." Our Lord warned that there is a peril in following disseminators of cognitive dissonance: "Let them alone: they be blind leaders of the blind. And if the blind lead the blind, both shall fall into the ditch" (Matt. 15:14, KJV).

Sadly, things got worse. For when pressed on the specific point of what "inadmissible" means as used in the proposed text, the responding bishop said: "To my mind, the pope maintains, and our version imitates, a certain, if you want, eloquent ambiguity on that point." Eloquent ambiguity. No bishop asked for further explanation and a silence fell on the room, like the silence when the sons of Noah covered their father's nakedness, but this time the shame was rhetorical. It was this writer's pleasure to have been a priest for William F. Buckley, who, like Newman's gentleman, was "merciful to the absurd." But had anyone described confused and potentially heretical thought as "eloquent ambiguity," Bill would have replied, as he did indeed to a guest on his *Firing Line* television program: "I won't insult your intelligence by suggesting that you really believe what you just said." To that we might add that executing a man is swifter and more humane than torturing him with clichés and hanging him with a frayed syllogism.

Our Peculiar Times

There is a time and place for ambiguity when it is an exercise of temperate expression. The ancient Greeks even had a deity or *daimon*, Sophrosyne, who represented a strength of character exemplified by discretion, circumspection, and restraint, according to Socrates in Plato's *Charmides*. But such venerable shrewdness is not the cynicism that cajoles bureaucrats into calculation for the sake of obfuscation and servile ambition. Significantly, when Sophrosyne escaped Pandora's box, she retreated to Mount Olympus, leaving the human race, including its clergymen, bereft of her guidance. "Sophrosyne," meaning moral sanity or restraint, was for Stoics such as Zeno one of the four chief virtues, and it remains a cardinal virtue for Christians. It is far different from ambiguity in the sense of obfuscation. That uncertain trumpet helps explain why 50 percent of millennial Catholics have left the Church, leaving her unprepared for battle (see 1 Cor. 14:8).

If "inadmissible" does not mean something essentially different from what has already been said magisterially about capital punishment, why is it necessary to revise the *Catechism* to include it? Secondly, if the word "inadmissible" is deliberately ambiguous, why does it belong in a catechism, whose purpose is to eschew ambiguity? After all, in a catechism, ambiguity is even more problematic than a prudential opinion. Thirdly, how can ambiguity be eloquent since the etymology of "eloquence" means "forcefully expressive" and "revelatory" and is thus the opposite of verbal camouflage?

Only the angels of light know what would happen if assemblies of bishops spoke, like the Lord, as having "authority and not as the scribes" (Mark 1:22). Or suppose the bishops operated on the dominical principle: "But let your communication be, Yea, yea; Nay, nay: for whatsoever is more than these cometh of evil" (Matt. 5:37, KJV). An incapacity for indignation at calculated ambiguity is the consequence of a bureaucratic culture that melds ayes and nays into maybes. At the Baltimore assembly, the bishops approved the eloquently ambiguous statement by a vote of 194 for and 8 against, with 3 abstentions. Perhaps they were thinking like Nancy Pelosi, who said of the Affordable Care Act: "We have to pass the bill so that you can find out what is in it." Years from now, whether the Church will have risen from her present slough of despondency to a shining new eminence, or lie battered in a heap of broken basilicas and quivering banalities, the wonderful question will be: "How was it that, at a meeting in 2019, almost all of the American bishops voted for something without knowing what it means?"

June 26, 2019

The Strange Case of Dr. Biden and Mr. Hyde

Bishop Miler Magrath (Maolmhuire Mag Raith) of Ireland (1523–1622) wrote his own epitaph for the tomb in Cashel where he was finally laid in his one hundredth year. The syntax is convoluted as was his life: "Here where I am placed I am not. I am not where I am not. Nor am I in both places, but I am in each." It was his way of recalling that he managed to be a Catholic bishop and a Protestant bishop at the same time. He started out as a Franciscan friar, schooled in Rome, and soon became bishop of Down and Connor, then Clogher before Cashel, exacting rents from all of them, and adding Waterford, Lismore, Killala, and Achonry to his sees, becoming rich, although his cathedral in Cashel was said to be a pigsty, and few of his people were aware of the existence of God. Although he maintained many Franciscan ties—albeit wearing armor as protection against sullen rent payers—he authorized the hunting down of Papist priests while also warning them ahead of time, operating as a sort of double agent. Amy O'Meara of Toomevara married him, but devoutly refused to eat meat on Fridays and reared their nine children as Catholics. Pope Gregory VIII finally excommunicated him, but Paul V legitimized his children.

Bishop Magrath's creative rationalizing brings to mind his contemporary in England, Simon Aleyn, who was unable to maintain the duplicity of practicing two religions at the same time. To retain his living as vicar of the leafy and affluent parish of Bray in Berkshire, he switched creeds to accommodate whichever might be the religion du jour of the reigning monarch. In his charming book of curiosities, *Worthies of England* (1662), Thomas Fuller wrote:

> The vivacious vicar [of Bray] living under King Henry VIII, King Edward VI, Queen Mary, and Queen Elizabeth, was first a Papist, then a Protestant, then a Papist, then a Protestant again. He had seen some martyrs burnt two miles off at Windsor and found this fire too hot for his tender temper. This vicar, being attacked by one for being a turncoat and an inconstant changeling, said, "Not so, for I always kept my principle, which is this — to live and die the Vicar of Bray."

This would inspire a caustic ballad that has from time to time been tailored to fit half a dozen other churchmen of different periods, but with similar qualities of adaptability:

> And this is law, I will maintain
> Unto my Dying Day, Sir.
> That whatsoever King may reign,
> I will be the Vicar of Bray, Sir!

There is a political parallel to this malleability in the former vice president, Joe Biden, who has decided to run for the presidency as a Catholic independent of the strictures of Catholicism. As vice president, he officiated at the civil "marriage" of two men in 2016, although he had voted for the Defense of Marriage Act in 1996. When he was exploring a run for the presidency in 2008, Biden famously said: "I will shove my rosary beads down the throat of any Republican who says I am not a Catholic." The bishop of Cashel and the vicar of Bray could not have said it more eloquently.

On June 5, Biden had a campaign spokesman reiterate his longstanding support of the Hyde Amendment, which, having been passed by Congress in 1977, prevented federal funding for abortions, save for pregnancies caused by rape or incest or considered dangerous to the life of the mother. Such provisions at the time were believed to be pragmatic for attaining passage of the bill. A day after affirming the Hyde Amendment, Biden gave a speech in Atlanta in which he repudiated the law, while simultaneously insisting that he was not rejecting his previous position on abortion funding, and added that he would make "no apologies for the last position." His overnight flip-flop brings to mind the agility with which Senator Kerry in 2004 explained his stance on a supplemental appropriation for military operations in Iraq and Afghanistan: "I actually did vote for the $87 billion before I voted against it." That was matched and perhaps surpassed by the leader of the Australian party One Nation, Pauline Hanson, who said in 2018 with reference to tax cut legislation: "I haven't flip-flopped, I said no originally, then I said yes, then I have said no and I've stuck to it." To assure anyone who might put a cynical gloss on Biden's reversal, one of his campaign officials, TJ Ducklo, said, "This is about health care, not politics."

In a flash of honesty, Bismarck said: "Politics is the art of the possible, the attainable — the art of the next best." No one can survive in public life if he naïvely denies that situations may require compromise and even reversals. I was fortunate to know Congressman Henry Hyde, who counted his amendment his greatest achievement and told interesting stories of what was involved in getting it passed. I also knew Judge Bork, who was slandered by the rancorous attacks of shameless senators, including Biden, who ranted as chairman of the Senate Judiciary Committee: "It appears to me that you are saying that the government has as much right to control a married couple's decision about choosing to have a child or not, as that government has a right to control the public utility's right to pollute the air." Both Hyde and Bork were aware of the art of the possible, but they also knew that when retractions and contradictions affect matters of life or death, accommodation takes on an ominous character.

In *The Strange Case of Dr. Jekyll and Mr. Hyde*, Robert Louis Stevenson wrote of another and very different, indeed opposite, Mr. Hyde, but his cryptic message was that Jekyll and Hyde are the same man, and conscience is the serum that frees one and restrains the other: "I [Dr. Jekyll] was still cursed with my duality of purpose; and as the first edge of my penitence wore off, the lower side of me, so long indulged, so recently chained down, began to growl for license. Not that I dreamed of resuscitating Hyde ... no, it was in my own person, that I was once more tempted to trifle with my conscience."

Biden was given an honorary doctorate from Trinity College Dublin in 2016, enriching his academic laurels, which were tenuous after he placed 75 out of 86 in his Syracuse University College of Law class, although he claimed to have been in the top half. But if politics is the art of the possible, one must expect artistic liberties. Drawing on, and perhaps exhausting, his information on Shakespeare, Biden said that his mistake regarding school grades, like his propensity for appropriating sources without attribution, is "much ado about nothing." Academic rankings are not assurances of intelligence; in fact, Mr. — that is, Dr. Biden told a voter during a campaign stop in New Hampshire in 1987: "I think I probably have a much higher IQ than you." Armed with such confidence, Biden has wrestled with his conscience like a Sumo wrestler, thudding against that "aboriginal vicar of Christ" and bouncing off. Free of constricting guilt, and unafraid of the foolish need for consistency that is the hobgoblin of those little minds with IQs less than his, Biden now presents himself to the public as a prodigy of rejuvenation. With hair thicker and teeth whiter, beyond the skill of frail Mother Nature, and armed with his lethal rosary, he is ready to lead America like an eager Boy Scout helping an unwilling lady across the wrong street.

The Bourbon Henry of Navarre, baptized Catholic but reared Protestant and the champion of a Huguenot army, became King Henry IV of France by cutting a deal: he would declare himself Catholic. An intemperate Catholic, François Ravaillac, thought that a threatened invasion of the Spanish Netherlands proved the insincerity of Henry's conversion, and assassinated him in 1610. Although King Henry had said, "Paris vaut bien une messe" — by his arcane calculation, Paris was worth a Mass — the Church has never canonized him. Less saintly is anyone who calculates that Washington, D.C., is worth more than a Mass.

June 12, 2019

The Mendacity of Public Officials

My grandfather's nickname was David Lloyd George because he looked and spoke rather like the man. I was three days old when the former prime minister died, on the day that would have been my late grandfather's birthday. After the Versailles Conference, where he had sat between Woodrow Wilson and Georges Clemenceau, Lloyd George commented on how he had fared: "Not badly, considering I was seated between Jesus Christ and Napoleon."

Wilson was the idealist, a bad habit he had picked up after generations of attenuated Kantian and Schleiermachian philosophizing; Clemenceau was anything but an idealist. To him, and also to Lloyd George, is attributed the quotation, which possibly first came from Bismarck, "He who is not a socialist at 19, has no heart. He who is still a socialist at 30, has no brain." This occasions a dark joke, darker in the stark light of present-day Venezuela, that before socialists had candles for lighting, they had used electricity.

As commentary on the paucity of history courses in our schools, we now have elected officials who recommend socialism as the economic template for our age. The state of New York has a congresswoman who proudly calls herself a socialist. She is a product of the state that a *Forbes* magazine survey ranks first among the fifty states in money spent on public schools, while placing twenty-second in the quality of its education.

Our Peculiar Times

Meanwhile, the junior U.S. senator from New York, Kirsten Gillibrand, attended a private school for girls in Troy, New York, and later studied at the same college I did. I graduated a generation earlier and can confidently state—as well as measure with calipers the classical curriculum—that my class was the last of that college's golden age, with Senator Gillibrand a harbinger of its twilight. Our debating team, the Forensic Union, frequently won the national championship, continuing a tradition of an earlier U.S. senator, Daniel Webster. In discourses and debates, Gillibrand seems not to have been trained in any quality of forensic logic or persuasion. As a consequence, her oratory is not amazing; it is a maze.

While experience cautions theologians against the quicksand of politics, politicians frequently rush into theological matters where angels fear to tread, as Senator Gillibrand did on May 29 in a broadcast on National Public Radio. She announced that the Church is wrong about abortion, same-sex "marriage," and the male priesthood. This puts her at odds with all the saints and Doctors of the Church as well as Jesus Christ. The latter sent His Holy Spirit on Pentecost to lead the Church into all truth, and it is hard to believe that He reversed Himself in the recent years of our republic. Since it is "impossible for God to lie" (Heb. 6:18, KJV), the Lord would be at a disadvantage were He to run for the Senate from New York. This now would be a trifling matter were it not for the fact that Senator Gillibrand tells Catholics that she is a Catholic. Nevertheless, she seems certain that the Church's teaching on essential dogmas is quixotic. As she put it: "And I don't think they're supported by the Gospel or the Bible in any way. I just—I don't see it, and I go to two Bible studies a week. I take my faith really seriously."

On various issues, Gillibrand has boasted regarding her "flexibility." This was evident in her positions on gun ownership. Running for Congress in 2008 from a district populated by hunters, she wrote: "I appreciate the work that the [National Rifle Association] does to protect gun owners' rights, and I look forward to working with you for many years." After enjoying as a representative a 100 percent approval rating from the NRA, she became a supple senator and soon switched mental gears, earning an "F" from that same NRA, which she then described as "the worst organization in the country." Such flexibility reminds one of Ramsay MacDonald, whom Churchill likened to the Boneless Wonder of Barnum's circus: "A spectacle too demoralizing and revolting for my young eyes."

This mendacity became bolder on June 2 in a televised Fox News "town hall" forum when she said that "infanticide doesn't exist." Thus she ignored the "late-term" abortion bill signed by Governor Cuomo on January 22, as he sat next to a smiling Sarah Weddington, who had been counsel to the lying, and later repentant, plaintiff in the *Roe v. Wade* case. In his own Senate days, Mr. Obama led the way as a paladin of infanticide. The governor of Virginia, Ralph Northam, who knows what he is talking about as a pediatric neurologist, admitted with insouciance: "If a mother is in labor, I can tell you exactly what would happen. The infant would be delivered. The infant would be kept comfortable. The infant would be resuscitated if that's what the mother and the family desired. And then a discussion would ensue between the physicians and the mother."

Like a rhetorical Houdini breaking free from the shackles of consistency, Gillibrand then defended a woman's "right to make a life and death decision." But if the unborn is not human and if nothing is killed, why speak of a need to decide between life and death? There is little difference between a slip of the tongue and a slip of the scalpel. Gillibrand's incoherence is not a mistake the Holy Spirit would have made, but her solecism does reek of the Father of Lies. The senator's rant was the equivalent of the action of a clumsy saboteur, not unlike Claudius in *Hamlet* fatally "hoist with his own petard."

Our Peculiar Times

On the same Sunday that Senator Gillibrand spoke at the "town hall forum," there was a ceremony in the Romanian town of Blaj. Pope Francis beatified seven Greek-Catholic bishops who were martyred between 1950 and 1970 after unspeakable tortures during the Communist dictatorship of Nicolae Ceaușescu. The Stalinesque autocrat had been hailed over the years as the "Genius of the Carpathians" by some Westerners because he posed as somewhat independent of the Kremlin, although one out of every thirty Romanians was under some sort of criminal custody or censorship, and one-fifth of the half-million concentration camp prisoners did not survive. According to Vatican News, the papal throne used during the Divine Liturgy was made from the wooden planks of the prison beds, and from the iron bars of the prison windows where some of the martyrs died. The seven bishops sacrificed their lives in defense of the Faith that Senator Gillibrand has said is flawed, unchristian, and unbiblical.

In the beatification homily, the pope warned against "new ideologies" that threaten to uproot people from their "richest cultural and religious traditions." There are "forms of ideological colonization that devalue the person, life, marriage, and the family" and the faithful must "resist these new ideologies now springing up." This was language that one does not often hear at such volume in Rome itself these days, but it may have been inspired by the Spirit of Truth who speaks through martyrs over the dissonance of bureaucrats and the stuttering of mediocrities. Because of their obedience to God who cannot lie, those Blessed Martyrs will never be known in the chronicles of history as Boneless Wonders.

June 5, 2019

Science and the Ascension of Christ

A legion of publishers will attest that Fr. Stanley Jaki (1924–2009) did not suffer fools gladly, and under that category he filed virtually all editors. He wrote in perfect English, but with a discernible Hungarian syntax, so that his footnotes could be longer than the main text, and verbs often were fugitive. His patience with anyone who corrected the smallest iota was that of General Hunyadi dealing with a Turk. But he inherited the same remnant Magyar bloodline that inspired, on occasion, Liszt and Mindszenty. There are those who rank this Benedictine priest among those palmary cleric-scientists who radically changed the way the world understands itself: Nicolaus Copernicus in astronomy; Gregor Mendel in genetics; Giuseppe Mercalli in seismology; and Georges Lemaître, who proposed a "first atomic moment," which detractors at first mocked as a "big bang." But when Arno Penzias and Robert Wilson detected background radiation and thus ushered in experimental cosmology, ridicule changed to astonishment.

So it was not only a challenge but also a privilege to have had Fr. Jaki as a mentor and friend for about twenty years, and I have recorded some of this in my book *Cloud of Witnesses*. Not even popes escaped his deft scalpel, and his opening words in our first conversation were a complaint about the new Polish pontiff, whom he already revered as a saint, but whose philosophizing he faulted for his Achilles' heel of phenomenology. As a dwarf on the shoulders of such giants, I was subject to correction from him for treating the big bang as a theological statement. I may take the tone of his words to my grave, but I learned from it, and in retrospect it was a pale version of the way Fr. Georges Lemaître, inventor of that "first atomic moment," politely corrected Pope Pius XII in 1951.

On November 22 of that year, the pope delivered a lengthy address to the Pontifical Academy of Science entitled "Proofs for the Existence of God in the Light of Modern Science." A month earlier, the Holy Father had given his memorable "Address to Midwives on the Nature of Their Profession." While he indulged a tendency to discourse on various subjects as a polymath, nevertheless what the pope said was as brilliant and as prophetic as Paul VI's encyclical *Humanae Vitae* published a quarter century later.

In the address on November 22, the pontiff did allow, with becoming modesty:

> It is quite true that the facts established up to the present time are not an absolute proof of creation in time, as are the proofs drawn from metaphysics and Revelation in what concerns simple creation or those founded on Revelation if there be question of creation in time. The pertinent facts of the natural sciences, to which We have referred, are awaiting still further research and confirmation, and the theories founded on them are in need of further development and proof before they can provide a sure foundation for arguments which, of themselves, are outside the proper sphere of the natural sciences.

But the title of the address was provocative, and he continued:

> Thus, with that concreteness which is characteristic of physical proofs, it has confirmed the contingency of the

universe and also the well-founded deduction as to the epoch when the cosmos came forth from the hands of the Creator. Hence, creation took place in time. Therefore, there is a Creator. Therefore, God exists! Although it is neither explicit nor complete, this is the reply we were awaiting from science, and which the present human generation is awaiting from it.

Neither the big bang nor Lemaître was mentioned, though other scientists were cited, and he almost certainly relied on the British mathematician Edmund Whittaker. We do not know who drafted the speech, but it did not satisfy Lemaître. It is not known whether he spoke personally in audience with the pope afterward or sent comments to him through others, but he made clear that with the best of intentions, the text was muddling physics with metaphysics, failing to respect their boundaries. Pius XII normally avoided sentimentality, and he disdained the confusing enthusiasm that can issue from imprudently speaking off the cuff, so he dropped the subject. In this he was as acute as John Paul II and Benedict XVI. Instead of wanting to make a mess, they sought ways to explain why the "Spirit of Truth" is not messy (see John 16:13). Pope John XXIII appointed Lemaître president of the Pontifical Academy, and Pope John Paul II furthered the discussion in a letter to the head of the Vatican Observatory in 1988:

It would entail that some theologians, at least, should be sufficiently well-versed in the sciences to make authentic and creative use of the resources that the best-established theories may offer them. Such an expertise would prevent them from making uncritical and overhasty use for apologetic purposes of such recent theories as that of the "Big Bang" in cosmology. Yet it would equally keep them from discounting altogether the potential relevance of such theories to the deepening of understanding in traditional areas of theological inquiry.

Einstein admired Lemaître and was docile when Lemaître did not shy from offering a corrective to his field equations of general relativity. You might say that Einstein, asserting that "God does not play dice," was agnostic about agnosticism. He said cryptically: "If God created the world, his primary concern was certainly not to make its understanding easy for us." Thinking more like Spinoza, he could be impatient with outright atheists: "The eternal mystery of the world is its comprehensibility." He would not say more without compromising the integrity of his own science. St. Augustine chartered the course centuries earlier: "We do not read in the Gospel that the Lord said, 'I will send the Paraclete to teach you the course of the sun and the moon'; in fact, He wanted to create Christians, not mathematicians." In the seventeenth century, Cardinal Baronius, a spiritual disciple of St. Philip Neri, epigrammed: "The Bible teaches us how one goes to heaven, not how the heavens go."

This applies to the enigmatic *Shekinah*, the presence of God, in the form of the cloud—*anan*—that accompanied the wandering Jews (Exod. 13:21) and appeared on Sinai (Exod. 24:16) and on Tabor (Matt. 17:5). Finally, the cloud—*nephele*—was seen at the Ascension (Acts 1:9). While this cloud could have been perceived by human senses, it was beyond physical analysis. Here meteorology yields to another dimension for which there is no human definition other than acknowledgement of its existence. The Christian response moves beyond analysis to rejoicing. When St. Paul spoke of a man who had experienced a "third Heaven" he could say no more than that (2 Cor. 12:2).

In the three accounts of the cloud at the Transfiguration, the apostles were "terrified," not at the brightness of the inexplicable light that shone from Christ, but at the way the light had the quality of darkness "when they entered the cloud." This was something from another dimension, a luminous darkness that St. John of the Cross experienced as a "dark night of the soul" and that previously St. Gregory of Nyssa struggled to express in words. Dionysius the Areopagite managed to say: "Those who would see God must pass beyond the limits of creation, into a state which is beyond human knowledge and light and speech, and must therefore, from the point of view of created beings, be called one of ignorance, darkness, and silence."

I knew a woman who, while Christmas caroling as a schoolchild, sang "Silent Night" outside Einstein's house at 112 Mercer Street in Princeton. The professor appeared on the porch with his violin and, while not singing the words, played the music. This scene might be an arresting illustration of Fr. Jaki's application of Gödel's incompleteness theorem to various attempts at formulating a "theory of everything."

In a sermon of the year 388, Gregory of Nyssa first referred to a special feast of the Ascension to celebrate the mysterious cloud predicted by the Psalmist. This was on the fortieth day; we lose the significance of time meeting eternity — *kronos* encountering *kairos* — when the feast is moved to the next Sunday for the convenience of hasty urban commuters and suburban shoppers.

At the Ascension, two men dressed in white asked: "Men of Galilee, why do you stand looking into heaven?" (Acts 1:11). What had been seen could not be comprehended by looking up, but it might have been apprehended by looking within, so they returned to the Temple. St. Paul drew on his own cosmology when he invoked the poem *Phaenomena* to show the deficiencies in the pantheism of its author Aratus, a Stoic, whose notion of an impersonal "life force" would be congenial to lax thinkers today (Acts 17:28). But having once been blinded by God's luminous presence, he proclaimed to those more inclined to consider what they know and what they do not know: "The Lord himself will descend from heaven.... And the dead in Christ will rise first; then we who are alive, who are left, shall be caught up together with them in the clouds to meet the Lord in the air; and so we shall always be with the Lord. Therefore comfort one another with these words" (1 Thess. 4:16, 17–18).

May 30, 2019

A Great Catch: The 153 Fish

"I welcome you on the eve of a great battle." So began General Dwight D. Eisenhower on May 15, 1944, solemnly addressing the admirals and generals and officers of the Allied Expeditionary Force, announcing the proposed strategy for Operation Overlord, codename for the Normandy invasion. Underestimated as an orator, Eisenhower riveted the attention of all in the tense atmosphere. The location was an unlikely one: a lecture hall of St. Paul's School in London. The boys had already been evacuated to Berkshire during the Blitz. The top brass, who had arrived from the advance command post of the supreme headquarters of the Allied forces at Southwick House in Hampshire, were seated on school chairs, with two armchairs occupied by King George VI and prime minister Winston Churchill. General Bernard Montgomery, the future field marshal, brought out his maps to show the British and American positions. The school served as headquarters of the Twenty-First Army Group under Montgomery, and he felt at home there because he was an Old Pauline. Planning took place in the office of his old headmaster, or high master, which was the title used from the day of the school's foundation in 1509 by John Colet.

As a close friend of Erasmus, and an even closer spiritual advisor to Thomas More, Colet was the epitome of a Renaissance humanist, laden with learning he had brought back from France and

Italy for lectures in his own university at Oxford. More lured him back to his birthplace of London where his father had been a rich merchant and twice lord mayor. As dean of St. Paul's Cathedral, Colet put his reforming principles to work with eloquent imprecations against the pride, concupiscence, covetousness, and worldly absorptions that had tainted the priesthood. Archbishop Warham of Canterbury dismissed frivolous charges of heresy brought against Colet by offended clerics. Colet's combination of charm and audacity engendered the respect even of Henry VIII, despite his bold preaching against the king's French wars. As a priest with no children of his own, and no nieces or nephews because all twenty-two of his siblings had died in childhood, Colet devoted much of his inherited fortune to founding St. Paul's School for teaching 153 boys literature, manners, and, with Renaissance flair, Greek on a par with Latin. Erasmus said that when Colet lectured he thought he was hearing a second Plato. If so, his Platonism was Christian. He wanted a great catch, like that of the 153 fish that the apostles had hauled in at the command of the Risen Christ. The boys would be welcome "from all nations and countries indifferently."

The catch was great indeed, and since then the school has turned out graduates including, just for starters: John Milton, Samuel Pepys, John Churchill, G. K. Chesterton, three holders of the Victoria Cross, and the astronomer for whom Halley's comet is named—all rising from the first 153.

Exegetes, sometimes with too much time on their hands, and even earnest saints, have teased 153 and other numbers into signifying possibly more than their meaning. Jerome tried to find some significance in the fact that the second-century Greco-Roman poet Oppian listed 153 species of fish in his 3,500 verses about fishing, the *Halieutica*, dedicated rather sycophantically to the emperor Marcus Aurelius and his son Commodus. Of course, Oppian was wrong in his counting; besides, he wrote after the compilation of the Gospels. Augustine found that 153 is the sum of the first seventeen integers, which may reveal nothing more than his skill at arithmetic. In his devotion to the Rosary, Louis de Montfort found something prophetic between the catch of Galilean fish and the sum of fifteen decades of the Hail Mary plus the first three beads.

There may be no end to such agile mental exercises, and I once wrote a book — *Coincidentally* — rather whimsically illustrating how it is possible to detect endless matrices if you try hard enough. For example, faddish New Age fascination with the esoteric numerology of Kabbalah cultism can strain minds. It may not have been a helpful influence on the popular singer who gave millions of dollars to a Kabbalah institute and recently was confined to a mental-health facility purportedly against her will. Carl Jung wrote at some length about what he termed "synchronicity" and warned that an obsession with "acausal principles" could unbalance reason. Yet even a detached observer might pause at the fact that the sacred Tetragrammaton appears 153 times in Genesis.

The point here is that there are many levels of meaning in divine revelation that may be clues to the operation of divine providence. "For I know the plans that I have for you, says the LORD, plans for welfare and not for evil, to give you a future and a hope" (Jer. 29:11). Even our limited mathematics may articulate something of the symmetry by which the pulse of creation may be taken: "To whom then will ye liken me, or shall I be equal? saith the Holy One. Lift up your eyes on high, and behold who hath created these things, that bringeth out their host by number" (Isa. 40:25–26, KJV). Perception of this saves the saints from madness and inspires them to awe.

Contemplation of the unity of the True God and True Man encounters layers of reality beyond the comprehension of human intelligence. Nonetheless, we can perceive the existence of those dimensions. A "participatory anthropic principle," first forwarded by John A. Wheeler, suggests that the universe is structured with a set of physical constants or "cosmic coincidences" without which there would be no intelligent life on earth, and that it is only by participating in that structure by rational perception that the constants or coincidences have their potency. So there may be in those 153 fish the Voice saying: "I have yet many things to say to you, but you cannot bear them now" (John 16:12).

It would be a mistake to suppose that the apostles went back to fishing, in disobedience to the Master's command years before to drop their nets and follow Him. Christ is the Alpha and Omega, meaning that He is able to know everything from start to finish at the same time. Before the Resurrection, Jesus told the apostles that they would meet a man in Jerusalem carrying a pitcher of water, from whom they would rent an upper room: "And they went, and found it as he had told them" (Luke 22:13). Thus He was also able to "set up" His men, ordering them to go to the Sea of Tiberius, knowing what He had prepared for them there, in order to instruct them.

In His humanity He did a domestic thing in cooking breakfast. In His divinity He predicted what the apostles would become. Whatever else may be encoded in the number 153, the fact is that this event happened, for had it been an oriental myth there would have been a million fish. This number was a detail never to be forgotten. Even when the youngest of them, the cadet of the Twelve, was the last to survive and his mind was weary with age, he said with a thrill like that of a youth: "That which was from the beginning, which we have heard, which we have seen with our eyes, which we have looked upon and touched with our hands, concerning the word of life" (1 John 1:1).

There is one thing we know that prevents miniaturizing Christ as the best of men but only a man: "For in him all things were created, in heaven and on earth, visible and invisible, whether thrones or dominions or principalities or authorities—all things were created through him and for him. He is before all things, and in him all things hold together" (Col. 1:16–17). In Him was an urgent appeal to the intellect, which for the Jew was a function of love and not confined to the brain, as is clear in the Resurrection appearance to Cleopas and his companion on the Emmaus road: "O foolish men, and slow of heart to believe all that the prophets have spoken! Was it not necessary that the Christ should suffer these things and enter into his glory?" (Luke 24:25–26). Here was the culmination of His earlier rabbinical catechesis:

"Having eyes do you not see, and having ears do you not hear? And do you not remember? When I broke the five loaves for the five thousand, how many baskets full of broken pieces did you take up?" They said to him, "Twelve." "And the seven for the four thousand, how many baskets full of broken pieces did you take up?" And they said to him, "Seven." And he said to them, "Do you not yet understand?" (Mark 8:18–21)

The unseen calculus that fascinated Oppian when counting fish in coastal Cilicia much more amazed William Blake when describing an imagined "Tyger," which certainly was not rampant in London: "What immortal hand or eye / Could frame thy fearful symmetry?" If there is substance to some anthropic principle in the play of numbers, it is found in the fact that after the 153 fish had been dragged to shore, a small fire was burning as Jesus asked Peter three times if he loved Him. And Peter wept in remembering that by another small fire in Jerusalem he had said three times that he never knew the Man.

May 17, 2019

What Newman Can Tell Us
about the Cardinal Pell Verdict[5]

The scene in the London courtroom in 1852 might have been out
of a Gilbert and Sullivan operetta, with the defendant in simple
clerical black standing in the dock before the bewigged representatives of ancient justice. But one of the judges, John Coleridge, a
great-nephew of the poet, saw behind the stooped figure of John
Henry Newman the shade of the Armada and the ghosts of spies
from Douai. Thus the trial of Newman was about more than the
slander of which he was accused. As a scion of Oxford, Coleridge,
whose own wife Jane Fortescue Seymour had painted a portrait of
Newman, resented that the Oxford Movement had been chipping
away at the claim of the Established Church to apostolic validity
and, worse, that it had become a halfway house to Rome.

Lord Campbell, who was the presiding judge, had authored
the Libel Act of 1843: "If any person shall consciously publish any
defamatory libel, knowing the same to be false, every such person,
being convicted thereof, shall be liable to be imprisoned in the

---

[5]   On April 7, 2020, a year after this essay was published, the seven
     judges of the High Court ruling for Brisbane unanimously acquit-
     ted Cardinal Pell.

common gaol or house of correction for any term not exceeding two years, and to pay such fine as the court shall award."

Newman had been arraigned under these provisions, for in a series of lectures on "The Present Position of Catholics in England," he had attracted large audiences, many of literary and political note, with an entertaining display of unfamiliar logic and eloquence during which he had delicately exposed the indelicacies of a defrocked Dominican friar of Naples: "A profligate under a cowl ... ravening after sin." One court reporter described the man: "He is a plain-featured, middle-sized man, about fifty years of age, and his face is strongly Italian. His forehead is low and receding, his nose prominent, the mouth and the muscles around it full of resolution and courage. He wears a black wig, the hair of which is perfectly straight, and being close shaved, this wig gives to his appearance a certain air of the conventicle. Yet he retains many traces of the Roman Catholic priest, especially in his bearing, enunciation, and features, which have a sort of stealthy grace about them. His eyes are deep-set and lustrous, and with his black hair, dark complexion, and somber, demure aspect, leaves an impression on the mind of the observer by no means agreeable, and not readily to be forgotten."

Giacinto Achilli, having fled the outraged fathers of various Italian maidens, justified his exploits by what he asserted was a correction of the Petrine claims. He hired himself out to an English No-Popery society called the Evangelical Alliance. The slowly emerging Catholic populace in England was inured to attacks by the crude and sophisticated alike, but it was intolerable to them that audiences were listening to the charmingly accented English of a Neapolitan friar who, having left a long line of defilements in his wake, including the rape of a fifteen-year-old girl in his church's sacristy on Good Friday, melodramatically described Rome as the whore of Babylon. He was forced to flee Malta after at least eighteen sexual offenses. His seductiveness took other forms, to the point of flattering the secretary for foreign affairs, Lord Palmerston, for his stilted Italian, which was fashionable in the age of the poetical Brownings, though inferior to the Italian of Newman's mercurial friend Gladstone. Cultural attitudes were stirred even more by the hysteria following the restoration of the Catholic episcopate to England and Wales in 1850, and Cardinal Wiseman did not help matters with his florid letter "From Out the Flaminian Gate," celebrating the fact. In the mind of the Anglican archbishop of York, Thomas Musgrave, this was "Rome's ever wakeful ambition plotting for our captivity and ruin."

The Achilli trial, as it came to be known, was one of the judicial dramas of the age. It would have had prime time on today's television. It began on June 21 in 1852 and lasted five days. One thinks of what the sensitive personality of Newman, whose whole life was consecrated to the "Kindly Light" of truth and whose youthful and aged boast was that he had never sinned against it, endured during the trial. Yet he was more than Stoic, because he was not a pagan Greek bowing to cruel fate but was luminously a son of serene truth. On the night of his conviction for libel against Achilli, secured after a neglectful Cardinal Wiseman had mislaid corroborative letters, he wrote unperturbed to a correspondent: "I could not help being amused at poor Coleridge's prose.... I think he wished to impress me. I trust I behaved respectfully, but he must have seen that I was as perfectly unconcerned as if I had been in my own room.... I have not been the butt of slander and scorn for 20 years for nothing."

Newman's legal team was comprised of some of the finest barristers in the land, headed by the colorful Sir Alexander Cockburn. He would serve as Lord Chief Justice from 1875 to 1880, though Queen Victoria refused him a peerage because of his louche private life.

Newman had been subjected to the condescension of Coleridge, who lamented Newman's "deterioration" from the heights of Protestantism. In his personal diary, Coleridge wrote: "Perhaps I have been so much accustomed to hear Newman's excellence talked of that I have received an exaggerated opinion of him. But I have a feeling that there was something almost out of place in my not merely pronouncing sentence on him, but in a way lecturing him.... Besides, in truth Newman is an over-praised man, he is made an idol of."

Newman was found guilty by the Queen's Bench and in the shocked aftermath even the *Times* observed: "We consider ... that a great blow has been given to the administration of justice in this country, and Roman Catholics will have henceforth only too good reason for asserting that there is no justice for them in cases tending to arouse the Protestant feelings of judges and juries." In the annals of jurisprudence, the Achilli trial helped to establish the bounds of the statutory defense of truth under the 1843 Libel Act.

It was a Pyrrhic victory for the Queen's Court and a moral victory for Newman—he had to pay a nominal fine of one hundred pounds but was not kept in custody. Court costs, nonetheless, were nearly the equivalent of two million dollars today, and the donations from home and abroad were a proclamation of universal Catholic solidarity. Newman saved letters from Boston, New York, Philadelphia, Baltimore, towns in the Midwest, and San Francisco. The year after the trial, Newman published his immortal *Idea of a University* and inscribed the volume:

> In grateful never-dying remembrance
> Of his many friends and benefactors,
> Living and dead,
> At home and abroad,
> In Great Britain, Ireland, France,
> In Belgium, Germany, Poland, Italy, and Malta,
> In North America, and other countries,
> Who, by their resolute prayers and penances,

And by their generous stubborn efforts
And by their munificent alms,
Have broken for him the stress
Of a great anxiety.

On November 26, Newman wrote reflectively to his sister Jemima: "I consider that the Judges did me a far greater injury than the Jury, for they made me incur the expense, and the long proceeding. I believe they are now much annoyed at the Verdict — but I cannot help saying that educated men and judges have more to answer for when they do wrong, than a vulgar, prejudiced jury."

It is hard to read those lines without consciousness of those many who now support the attestations of George Cardinal Pell as he stands in the vortex of a cultural tempest malignant in motive and design, preparing to appeal his conviction and sentence of six years in custody, handed down on March 13.[6] Theirs is the assurance from the apostolic fathers familiar with indictments and assaults, that those who endure will by their humiliations produce an abundant harvest. Anti-Catholic hysteria, not unlike that which preceded Newman's trial, animated charges against Cardinal Pell, indicting him for alleged profane acts witnessed by no one, which would have been impossible under the circumstances. Etymologists have traced the term "kangaroo court" to the makeshift jurisprudence of an Australian immigrant in the United States at the time of the 1849 gold rush — but Australia is the homeland of the marsupial. Cardinal Pell stood against politically correct policies such as contraception, abortion, the Gnostic revision of sexuality, and attempts to teach anthropogenic climate-change theories as

---

[6] Catholic News Agency, "Cardinal Pell Sentenced to Six Years Imprisonment for Sexual Abuse," *National Catholic Register*, March 12, 2019, https://www.ncregister.com/daily-news/cardinal-pell-sentenced-to-six-years-imprisonment-for-sexual-abuse.

dogma. These are not welcome opinions in the courts of secular correctness. He also began with unprecedented vigor, not typical in Rome, the task of cleaning the Augean stable of Vatican finances.

The situation now is different from 1852, because George Pell was accused and back then John Henry Newman was at first the accuser. But both subjects have claim to impeccable integrity, as well as being victims of justice miscarried. In the nineteenth century, Giacinto Achilli fled with his ruined reputation to the United States, having abandoned an acknowledged wife and son and at one point threatening suicide after some time in a utopian "free love" community in Oneida, New York. His grave has no marker, for his end is unknown. This year, by divine grace and mortal assent, Newman will be raised to the altars.

From a higher bar of consummate justice, Newman has the last word:

> What is good, endures; what is evil, comes to naught. As time goes on, the memory will simply pass away from me of whatever has been done in the course of these proceedings, in hostility to me or in insult, whether on the part of those who invoked, or those who administered the law; but the intimate sense will never fade away, will possess me more and more, of the true and tender Providence which has always watched over me for good, and of the power of that religion which is not degenerate from its ancient glory, of zeal or God, and of compassion towards the oppressed.

March 14, 2019

Comfort My People

The name of the stepbrother of William the Conqueror was a palindrome, and the ladies who made the Bayeux Tapestry must have enjoyed embroidering it along with the caption under the scene of Odo at the Battle of Hastings. A year after the Norman Conquest, he became duke of Kent, assuming vast lands and power, but William had already seen to it that he had been made a bishop at about the age of nineteen. He was serious about his episcopal office—even at Hastings, where a servant carried his crozier into the fray. Careful of the canonical prohibition against clerics' wielding a sword, he used a heavy club, and with it he threatened those among his troops who were reluctant to run headlong into the hail of arrows. The inscription on the tapestry, which he probably intended for his own cathedral, reads in abbreviated Latin: "Hic Odo Eps [Episcopus] Baculu[m] Tenens Confortat Pueros," which is to say, "Here, Bishop Odo, holding his club, comforts his boys." In our vernacular, this is not the sort of comfort one wants, but the word originally and essentially means "to strengthen." Derived from it are words such as "fortress" and "fortitude," the latter being one of the Seven Gifts of the Holy Spirit. This is the other Comforter that Christ promised, in order to "put on the whole armour of God, that ye may be able to stand against the wiles of the devil" (John 14:16; Eph. 6:11, KJV).

The equivalent for Comforter is Paraclete, or Advocate, which means "a strengthener who stands by the side of another" to plead on his behalf in a court of justice (cf. John 14:26; 15:26; 16:7; 1 John 2:1). This teaching comes from the Beloved Disciple, the object and bestower of singular tenderness. But he was not sentimental, for sentimentalism is sham love without sacrifice. St. John was strong enough to stand with Our Lady and comfort her at the Crucifixion after the older apostles had fled. The Beloved Apostle says in his second letter, and reiterates in his third, that those who are not faithful to the truth should be separated from those who are. "If any one comes to you and does not bring this doctrine, do not receive him into the house or give him any greeting; for he who greets him shares his wicked work" (2 John 1:10–11). By so saying, he does not slip into sentimentalism, and he prefigures the dictum of St. John Paul II in a general audience of November 8, 1978, that "there is no love without justice." A few years earlier, Archbishop Fulton Sheen phrased it thus: "Justice without love could become tyranny, and love without justice could become toleration of evil." That pastiche of love claims to feel your pain while inflicting it, and comforts you while destroying you.

Few verses in all literature match St. Paul's hymn to love (1 Cor. 13). But to cherry-pick the apostle's words in order to show God's mercy, to the exclusion of what he says earlier, is to emasculate his exaltation of sacrificial love: "What have I to do with judging outsiders? Is it not those inside the church whom you are to judge? God judges those outside. 'Drive out the wicked person from among you.'" (1 Cor. 5:12–13). Had Paul demurred from speaking truth to Caesar in the hope of bringing him to a better frame of mind and parading with him on festive days through the Forum, he might have kept his head, at least for a while.

These thoughts came to mind when the governor of Virginia was attacked from all sides for allegations of racism, an offense against human dignity, while his publicly avowed permission to kill babies born as well as unborn has been neuralgically downplayed. Grounds for demanding his resignation were not based on infanticide, but on his sophomoric prancing about in blackface. The media overwhelmingly demurred from commenting on the governor's justification of infanticide, saying one way or another that they did not have enough facts. Such lack did not prevent them from ranting against some racially demeaning yearbook photographs of him with another figure dressed as a Klansman. The media have given that more publicity in a few days than they ever gave a photograph of Planned Parenthood founder Margaret Sanger addressing the Ku Klux Klan. This image is said to have been "photoshopped," but Sanger did address a women's branch of the Klan in Silver Lake, New Jersey, albeit uncomfortably, and she minced no words about her eugenics.

As a pediatric neurologist, Governor Northam spoke with clinical detachment about "comforting" babies who survive abortion: "The infant would be delivered. The infant would be kept comfortable. The infant would be resuscitated if that's what the mother and the family desired. And then a discussion would ensue between the physicians and the mother." He did not explain what the discussion would include, but, in contemporary America, it certainly would echo the moral desolation and self-inflicted punishment of depraved Babylon: "They will have no mercy on the fruit of the womb; their eyes will not pity children" (Isa. 13:18). As for medical qualifications, and prescinding from imputations of absolute equivalence, it is sobering to recall that Josef Mengele had degrees in anthropology and medicine (cum laude) from the Universities of Munich and Frankfurt, and worked as an abortionist in Brazil after the war, as did Vilis Kruze, an SS officer and physician, in

Our Peculiar Times

Ohio and Hawaii. Abortionists seem to have an international and ageless fraternity of their own.

Governor Northam's kind of comfort was not that of Bishop Odo prodding his troops, for it was rather in the line of sedation before annihilation, and a nursery version of Otto von Bismarck's protocol: "Every courtesy as far as the gallows."

Justin Fairfax, lieutenant governor of Virginia, is a former Planned Parenthood official and is even more aggressively pro-infanticide than Northam. For all of their ilk, when it comes to "comfort," they are like scornful Humpty Dumpty:

> "When I use a *word*, it *means* just what I *choose* it to *mean* —neither more nor less."
>
> "The question is," said Alice, "whether you can make *words mean* so many different things."
>
> "The question is," said Humpty Dumpty, "which is to be master—that's all."

There are those of intractable moral confusion who would vote for those whose mastery of words removes the adverb "not" from the commandments of God.

Confounding attempts to pigeonhole the abortion scandal as a moral tumult only in the minds of Catholics, other voices from different platforms have condemned abortion, including John Calvin who was anything but a friend of Catholicism:

> The unborn, though enclosed in the womb of his mother, is already a human being, and it is an almost monstrous crime to rob it of life which it has not yet begun to enjoy. If it seems more horrible to kill a man in his own house than in a field, because a man's house is his most secure place of refuge, it ought surely to be deemed more atrocious to destroy the unborn in the womb before it has come to light. (Commentary on Exod. 21:22)

The moral probity of killing an infant after birth was beneath consideration.

At the ordination of a bishop, a book of the Gospels is placed on the head the bishop-elect, for he is to be subservient to the Word of God in order to serve the People of God. There have been admirable bishops who edify by the simple clarity of their discipline. Among them is Bishop Thomas Daly, who wrote in a pastoral letter of February 1, 2019: "Politicians who reside in the Catholic Diocese of Spokane, and who obstinately persevere in their public support for abortion, should not receive Communion without first being reconciled to Christ and the Church."[7]

Vacuous comforters may cajole their flocks with congenial platitudes, but there is no strength in this. (*Risus abundat in ore stultorum*: "Fools are full of laughter.") There is a long line of those who confuse sycophancy with prophecy, whose operative ambition is their own comfort and the solace of approval by those who are as superficial as they are. "Again I saw all the oppressions that are practiced under the sun. And behold, the tears of the oppressed, and they had no one to comfort them! On the side of their oppressors there was power, and there was no one to comfort them" (Eccles. 4:1).

February 7, 2019

---

[7] JD Flynn, "Bishop Daly: Pro-Choice Pols Should Not Receive Eucharist," Catholic News Agency, February 2, 2019, https://www.catholicnewsagency.com/news/bishop-daly-pro-choice-pols-should-not-receive-eucharist-97896.

Governor Cuomo's Bridge

There was a literary symbiosis between G. K. Chesterton and Henri Ghéon somewhat like the musical one between Rimsky-Korsakov and Mussorgsky. Ghéon's biography of St. John Vianney, *The Secret of the Curé d'Ars*, is enhanced by the brief commentary that Chesterton added to it. Chesterton mentions a mayor of some French town who not only commissioned a statue of the rationalist Émile Zola, but, intent on further provocation, ordered that the bronze for it be forged from the bells of a church. This rings a bell, if you will, when we are reminded that an ecstatic Governor Andrew Cuomo chose to sign into law our nation's most gruesome abortion bill on January 22, the anniversary of the *Roe v. Wade* decision, to raucous applause and cheering in the state capitol. In a fallen world, dancing on graves requires no instructors. Then Cuomo ordered that One World Trade Center in Manhattan and the Alfred E. Smith Building in Albany be illuminated in pink. The ancient Caesars dressed in red as the token of victory. Cuomo chose pink.

Mark the ironies: the Freedom Tower is at the site of the memorial to the dead of 9/11, and listed on that somber shrine are eleven "unborn babies" killed with their mothers. As for Al Smith's building, that chivalric Catholic personality would have resigned rather than endorse infanticide.

Our Peculiar Times

In Orwellian "newspeak," just as a concentration camp is called a "joycamp," the killing of innocent unborn infants is sanctioned by New York's "Reproductive Health Act." This macabre euphemism declares that it is legal to destroy a fully formed baby seconds before birth and, should it survive a botched attempt to cut it up, attendants are allowed to let it die. The abortionist does not even need to be a medical doctor. Under certain conditions an ambiguously defined "authorized practitioner" might qualify.

The legislation was deferred over the years by politicians who, if not paragons of empathy, were appalled by its excess. It has passed only because the Democrats now control both houses of the New York state legislature. Politics aside, the governor teased a religious question. Not only did he mention that he was once an altar boy, but he concluded the signing celebration by praying for the legislators: "God bless you." It was an echo of the time that Barack Obama invoked God's blessings over a national gathering of Planned Parenthood. A popular singer, Charlie Daniels, was so taken aback by this that he tweeted: "The NY legislature has created a new Auschwitz dedicated to the execution of a whole segment of defenseless citizens. Satan is smiling." Theologians may differ as to whether the Prince of Darkness can laugh, but he certainly can smile as a way of showing that, in a Miltonian sense, evil is his good. Meanwhile, the bleak visage of Governor Cuomo should be shielded from children allowed to live, for it resembles with each declining day a grotesque icon of the Giver of Life in reverse.

From his rambling rhetoric, untutored diction, and scant intellectual formation, we may assume that Governor Cuomo has escaped the brush of Lord Acton's aphorism that power tends to corrupt, and absolute power corrupts absolutely. Cuomo's power may not be absolute, although it has now proven deadly, but even power that is not absolute enjoys a blithe courtship with vice. His official website now displays the cook with whom he shares a home in a relationship that would have exercised John the Baptist. This has barred him from Holy Communion as a disciplinary norm, if not a canonical penalty, and in recent times he has observed this. But, as a preeminent canon lawyer, Dr. Edward Peters, has indicated, Cuomo's communicant status is further impeded by Canon 915 because of his promotion of the "Reproductive Health Act." Dr. Peters says: "Penal jurisdiction in this matter rests with the bishop of Albany (as the place where some or all of the canonically criminal conduct was committed, per Canon 1412), and/or with the archbishop of New York (as the place where Cuomo apparently has canonical domicile, per Canon 1408)." Canonical discipline should not be caricatured as a "weapon," since it is properly punitive to promote justice and prevent scandal, as well as medicinal to reform and safeguard the spiritual state of the offender.

These matters are beyond the ken or jurisdiction of a parish priest, but it is clear that it is not sufficient for churchmen blithely to suppose that an adequate response to the massacre of innocents by the inversion of reason merits nothing more than an expression of "profound sadness." The faithful are entitled to the expectation that their bishops will qualify as vertebrates in more than a purely anthropological sense. Our Lord did not chase the moneychangers out of His Father's house with a whimper of melancholy.

Although our Founding Fathers rejected a hereditary form of government, it roams like a ghost through various corridors of state. One is hard pressed to convince people that Andrew Cuomo would be presiding in Albany had his father not formerly occupied his seat. Just as Andrew engages a reverie of his days as an altar boy, so Mario invoked his membership in the Legion of Mary. However, Mario rightly resented any imputation of a family connection to the Mafia. He is to be credited for his familial piety. This writer was a good friend of Mario Cuomo's predecessor, Governor Hugh Carey, and I can attest that Carey much regretted not having blocked an abortion bill during his tenure. But when Carey was out of office and devoting himself to pro-life witness, he was hounded and threatened about this by his successor Mario in a way redolent of *The Godfather*.

Perhaps Andrew Cuomo is succumbing to the temptation that some of the senators of classical Rome detected as evidence of decadence: the apotheosis, or divinizing, of emperors in an imperial cult complementary to the traditional deities. Ignoring the objections of more than one hundred thousand petitioners, Andrew named the Tappan Zee replacement bridge over the Hudson River in honor of his father. The Romans also developed the custom of *damnatio memoriae*, which erased the memory of disfavored predecessors. This fate was dealt out to twenty-six of the emperors before Constantine. The Egyptians did something similar when they erased the memorials of the pharaohs Hatshepsut and Akhenaten. In like fashion, Andrew Cuomo eliminated the name of former governor Malcolm Wilson from the old bridge, which was blown up last month.

In dark ages, there was a superstition that a bridge would be safe only if sacrificial victims, preferably children, were buried in its foundations. Peter Ackroyd mentions this in his history of London; it was more than a legend, as a child's body was found in the foundation of the Bridge Gate at Bremen. It was a ritualized practice in Japan, called *hitobashira*. If Andrew Cuomo persists in ignoring the petitions of the people of Rockland and Westchester Counties, and keeps the name of his father for the duration of the construction, there will be enough sacrificed bodies, all of them innocents, to ensure the soundness of the Mario Cuomo Bridge. Herod Antipas could not have been prouder of his father (who did not enjoy a good reputation in Bethlehem).

One theory is that some Church leaders have been reluctant to annoy Governor Andrew Cuomo in the midst of civil investigations of the Church, given the recriminatory personality of the man. But accommodation is a weak strategy. After the Munich Agreement, Winston Churchill said, "And do not suppose that this is the end. This is only the beginning of the reckoning. This is only the first sip, the first foretaste of a bitter cup which will be proffered to us year by year unless by a supreme recovery of moral health and martial vigor, we arise again and take our stand for freedom as in the olden time." Corroborating that warning, just days after his "Reproductive Health Act," on January 28, Andrew Cuomo "celebrated" the passage through the state senate of the "Child Victims Act" aimed at Catholic institutions.

While contemplating the Crucified Christ, Doctors of the Church have seen His flesh as paper, His blood as ink, and the nails as pens. So the Word of God is blotted out by the words of the morally illiterate. After Governor Cuomo signed the "health" act, he handed his pen—having driven the nail into Christ—to a grinning and grandmotherly woman whose ample lap could have held several children. Alas, she had none.

January 30, 2019

Infamous Scribblers:
Virtue-Signalers on the Warpath

From October 22 to November 30, in 1878, a large fair was held in the Cathedral of St. Patrick in New York City before its dedication. It took advantage of the magnificent open space before pews were installed to the distress of the architect, James Renwick, who objected that Protestant furniture had no place in a Catholic shrine. Renwick was a Protestant himself, but also an aesthetic purist and an Anglican, and no Puritan; however, Archbishop McCloskey needed money and, as with having a fundraising fair, renting pews out was a way to get it.

Six months earlier, and exactly one block north in her huge mansion on the same side of Fifth Avenue, Madame Restell had reclined in her bathtub and slit her throat. She left a fortune of over twelve million dollars in today's money, after a career as the nation's most notorious abortionist. Not unfamiliar with prison, she had been haunted throughout her dismal career by what we would now call investigative journalists in the employ of the *New York Times*. Founded in 1851, the "Gray Lady" became the journal of the new Republican Party and helped with the demolition of the corrupt Tweed Ring.

Times change, even for the *New York Times*, which over more recent years has abandoned its foundational moral rectitude.

Our Peculiar Times

Although not proud of its whitewashing of the Ukraine famine and Stalin's show trials by the complicit reporter Walter Duranty, the newspaper has not yet renounced his Pulitzer Prize, nor has it demurred from the praise heaped on it by Fidel Castro when he visited its editorial office in a gesture of thanks for the paper's support. There was also that problem with Jayson Blair's plagiarism, and the misrepresentation of the young men falsely accused of sexual violence at Duke University. The latter bears some resemblance to the recent incident in our nation's capital when youths from Covington Catholic High School were accused of racist bullying. But the *New York Times* has had the decency, along with some others, to regret the haste with which it moved to condemn the innocent.

Unlike Mark Twain, who noted that reports of his death were greatly exaggerated, those who now say that journalism is dead may have a good case. Thus one should not expect much from those who report the activities of others and by so doing arrogate to themselves the importance of the actors. Despite the fact that he was a journalist himself, G. K. Chesterton said that writing badly is the definition of journalism.

When hieroglyphics were the best, if static, medium of telling the news in the thirteenth century B.C., Rameses the Great advertised himself as the victor of the Battle of Kadesh, although truth-tellers knew that he had lost. The city of Trent spread a "blood libel" against Jews in 1475 that led to a massacre, and not even Pope Sixtus IV could stop it, though he tried. In 1765, Samuel Adams, whose only worthy legacy is beer, falsely claimed in print that Thomas Hutchinson, a Loyalist, supported the Stamp Tax, with the result that the helpless man's house was burned to the ground. In 1782, five months after Yorktown, Benjamin Franklin produced a hoax news release during his sojourn in Paris, claiming that King George had induced American Indians to commit atrocities, and he also forged the name of John Paul Jones to another libel. And, of course, Marie Antoinette never said "Let them eat cake" (actually it was "brioche"), but those who wanted to believe it did so. George Washington had enough of journalists, and told Hamilton that he was quitting public life because of "a disinclination to be longer buffitted [sic] in the public prints [sic] by a set of infamous scribblers."

There is no need to recount the details of the latest incident in our nation's capital, when the high school boys were defamed by journalists with the accusation that they mocked an elderly American Indian who was trying to calm a confrontation with a radical group of anti-white, anti-Semitic racists. Videos proved that there was no truth to this, but a flurry of demagogic "virtue signaling" berated the boys without giving them a chance to testify. In the eyes of the secular media, the lads were at a portentous disadvantage, being white Catholic males, some of whom were wearing MAGA hats. The "American Indian" was described as an elderly Vietnam War veteran. But few sixty-four-year-olds today would qualify as geriatric. And in the last year that any U.S. combat units were stationed in Vietnam — 1973 — he would have been eighteen years old. Mr. Phillips, a professional "activist" for the Indigenous Peoples March, also claims to be a marine veteran, which may be the case, but to have been a marine in Vietnam when the last marine combat divisions left in 1971, he would have been sixteen years old. This information has been ignored in some quarters. Journalists were supposed to expose hoaxes pretending to be facts, but now they prefer to call facts hoaxes. I speak without prejudice; having been born in New Jersey, I can also claim to be an indigenous person. Besides that, as a teenager, I was schooled in a college originally established for the education of Indians, as they were once universally called.

This brings up a contiguous complaint. As soon as this incident was reported, the *Washington Post*, in its role as the intemperate sibling of the *New York Times*, ran an essay decrying "the shameful exploitation of Native Americans by the Catholic Church." For secularists, any missionary venture must have been exploitative and destructive of Native culture, even though Christian evangelists have thwarted infanticide, human sacrifice, the cremation of widows, polygamy, caste systems, and, yes, slavery. The article in the *Post* made no mention of the Jesuit martyrs who endured torture and death to bring the gospel to dejected tribes and peace to internecine tribal slaughterers. Absent was mention of St. Kateri Tekakwitha, who was exiled by her own tribe, the Mohawks, for her love of Christ; St. Junipero Serra, who transformed the fortunes of the indigenous "gatherer" culture; St. Katharine Drexel, who donated her vast inheritance to establish fifty missions among the Native peoples; the heroic bishop Martin Marty, who brought science and literacy to the Dakota Territory; or Fr. Pierre-Jean de Smet, who fashioned the Fort Laramie Treaty of 1868, and so befriended Chief Tatanka Iyotake ("Sitting Bull") that the venerable chief, impeded from his own reception into the Church by having two wives, wore a crucifix to his dying day and saw to it that Buffalo Bill Cody was baptized the day before he died. Defamation by journalists is unethical in the professional sphere and sinful in the economy of God, but to submit saints to detraction is blasphemous.

The scene of Pope Leo XIII applauding the Wild West show of Buffalo Bill and Chief Sitting Bull on tour in Rome would probably confound journalists at the *Washington Post*. Buffalo Bill and his entourage were wined and dined at the North American College there, an event that might have been inaccurately reported by CNN. But these are facts, and Catholics who do not know their history are accountable for letting it be maligned.

The incident with the Covington boys may be more significant than some transient scandal. One remembers Senator Joseph Mc-Carthy's using the media to his advantage, and to this day his foes will not admit that he did indeed expose some real threats to the nation. The young Robert Kennedy was his assistant attorney, and McCarthy was godfather to Robert's first daughter, Kathleen, although he died four years later and obviously had no catechetical influence. But when McCarthy's actions became extravagant, the U.S. Army attorney Joseph Welch asked, "Have you no sense of decency?" Therewith the whole deck of cards collapsed. Perhaps the media are beyond a sense of shame now, wallowing as they are in destructive polemics, but fair-minded people may be moved by this Covington incident to recognize the indecency of political correctness. Such correctness is most demeaning when it cloaks itself in an affected moralism that agnostic subjectivism has otherwise displaced from social discourse.

Our Lord condemned "virtue signaling" in His parable of the Pharisee and the tax collector in the Temple. "I thank you, Lord, that I am not like this sinner" (see Luke 18:11). There are Pharisees in every corridor of society, but they find a most comfortable berth in the Church. So it was that the very diocese of the Covington students, without interviewing them or asking for evidence outside the media, promptly threatened to punish them. There was no mention of the hateful racism and obscene references to priests chanted by the cultic Hebrew Israelites as they threatened those Catholic youths. Instead, bishops issued anodyne jargon about the "dignity of the human person" without respecting the dignity of their own spiritual sons. The latest advertisement of the Gillette razor company portraying examples of "toxic masculinity" did not accuse any bishop, but only ecclesiastical bureaucrats would consider that a compliment. Pope Francis, off the cuff and at a high altitude in an airplane, once asked, "Who am I to judge?" There might at last be some application of that malapropism to shepherds who jump to judgment and throw their lambs to the wolves of the morally bankrupt media in a display of virtue signaling and in fear of being politically incorrect.

January 23, 2019

A Nursery Rhyme Pope Francis
Would Do Well to Read

"Will you walk into my parlour?" said the Spider to the Fly,
" 'Tis the prettiest little parlour that ever you did spy;
The way into my parlour is up a winding stair,
And I've a many curious things to shew when you are there."

Mary Howitt wrote 180 books with her husband and was a friend
of Wordsworth and Dickens, but is remembered perhaps most of all
for her children's parable about insects, written in 1828. She forsook
her ardent Quaker roots sometime after moving to Rome, where
she became a Catholic, less because of the Latin culture and more
for her admiration of Pope Leo XIII and his social commentaries.
She admitted that she loved the pope and not the papacy.

Combine her Spider and Fly with Our Lord's admonitions about
sheep among wolves, and serpentine cleverness with dovelike innocence, and we have a whole menagerie as commentary on naïveté.
It is possible to combine all the tragedies of the modern age into
a montage of the perils of unwitting ignorance in the face of evil.

The spectacle of Neville Chamberlain standing in an unprecedented protocol between the king and queen on the balcony of
Buckingham Palace in 1938, being cheered for having secured
"peace for our time" — *horresco referens* — is not the proudest

moment in modern royal history. But on the appeaser's death two years later, Churchill, with characteristic chivalry, paid him a tribute in the House of Commons:

> Whatever else history may or may not say about these terrible, tremendous years, we can be sure that Neville Chamberlain acted with perfect sincerity according to his lights and strove to the utmost of his capacity and authority, which were powerful, to save the world from the awful, devastating struggle in which we are now engaged. This alone will stand him in good stead as far as what is called the verdict of history is concerned.

It remains that the verdict of history is more acclamatory regarding Chamberlain's successor. While there is some confusion as to whether Churchill, in January 1940, as First Lord of the Admiralty, precisely said that an appeaser hopes that if he feeds the crocodile enough, he will be the last to be eaten, he did say verbatim: "Appeasement in itself may be good or bad according to the circumstances. Appeasement from weakness and fear is alike futile and fatal." This is reminiscent of divine words: "For the simple are killed by their turning away, and the complacence of fools destroys them" (Prov. 1:32).

Posterity was not well served by the manner in which Franklin Roosevelt found humor in the verbal gymnastics between Stalin and Churchill at Yalta, the latter being treated as a fly by both Stalin and FDR. That searing moment in history was not overlooked by the author of the encyclical *Centesimus Annus*, who came from the Poland that had been crucified by the moral lassitude of FDR and his "Uncle Joe." There would be a flashback to Lincoln Steffens's saying of the Soviet Union that he had seen the future and it worked, and to George Bernard Shaw clutching a small statue of Stalin. And then there would be Helmut Schmidt's recollection of a conversation he had had about the Berlin Wall with the be-nighted Jimmy Carter: "Then, I realized how little my counterpart understood of the situation in a divided Europe and the power of the Soviet Union and its interests."

Adroit diplomacy secures amity, but at its worst it lets loose ministers who are innocent as serpents and wise as doves. Charles de Gaulle, who was not subtle, said: "Diplomats are useful only in fair weather. As soon as it rains, they drown in every drop." Without succumbing to cynicism, one can see a mixture of calculation and callowness in the 2018 provisional agreement between the Holy See and Communist China, recognizing the primacy of the pope, but at the price of a scandalously clandestine arrangement giving the Chinese government a role in the appointment of bishops. This is in direct abuse of Canon 377.5 in the Church's own code.

Ever since Constantine, and certainly since Pope Leo III crowned Charlemagne in 800, ecclesiastical and civil threads have been intertwined. The medieval investiture controversies were the background for the sixteenth-century appointment privileges granted to the French crown and the nineteenth-century concordat between Pius VII and Napoleon. In the year that Mary Howitt wrote about the Spider, nearly five of every six bishops in Europe were appointed by heads of state. Right into modern times, Spain and Portugal invoked the *Patronato Real* and the *Padroado* respec-tively, but these involved governments that were at least nominally Catholic. The 1933 *Reichskonkordat* with the Nazi government was soon recognized as a maladroit concession for which the Holy See continues to justify itself. But Pius XI honored the Faith with his subsequent condemnations of fascism. The Vatican's accom-modationist Ostpolitik in the 1960s made Cardinal Mindszenty a living martyr. The Second Vatican Council sought, largely suc-cessfully, to reserve the appointment of bishops to the sovereign pontiff (*Christus Dominus*, no. 20). But this was also in the context of an agreement with Russian Orthodox observers—and therefore obliquely with the Soviet government—that the Council would never mention communism, history's worst oppressor of Christians, by name. It was a jejune exercise in diplomacy, sterile in result, and remedied only by figures who rejected such supinity: John Paul II, Ronald Reagan, and Margaret Thatcher.

The mellow response of the People of God to the recent canonization of Pope Paul VI is in significant contrast to the reaction of many to the diplomatic betrayal of Cardinal Mindszenty in 1974.[8] After years of heinous torture, the primate of Hungary asked the papal secretary of state, Cardinal Villot: "Why do you appoint bishops in the countries of the Eastern bloc? It would be better if there were none, rather than those whom the governments allow you to appoint." When Mindszenty refused to renounce his see of Esztergom and the primacy, Paul VI declared his jurisdictions vacant, informing the "white martyr" of this on November 18, 1973. The cardinal said it was a crucifixion worse than his physical tortures. Upon Villot's retirement in 1979, Cardinal Casaroli succeeded him, pursuing the same Ostpolitik. This writer remembers graffiti in Rome during this period: "Mindszenty Si. Casaroli No." There is a poignant conundrum today: Paul VI has just been canonized, and mention of Mindszenty remains mute.

It was my privilege to know Cardinal Ignatius Kung Pin-Mei of Shanghai, who endured thirty years in prison, and Archbishop Dominic Tang Yee-Ming of Canton who was imprisoned for twenty-two years, seven of them in solitary confinement. The retired cardinal archbishop of Hong Kong, Joseph Zen, sees a betrayal of those

---

[8] Paul Kengor, "Pope Francis and the Cardinal Mindszenty Treatment in China," *Crisis Magazine*, February 12, 2018, https://www.crisismagazine.com/2018/pope-francis-cardinal-mindszenty-treatment-china.

who have suffered so much for Christ. Time will tell if the present diplomacy is wise. An architect of the Holy See's agreement with Communist China, Cardinal Parolin, said: "The Church in China does not want to replace the state, but wants to make a positive and serene contribution for the good of all." His words are drowned out by the sound of bulldozers knocking down churches while countless Christians languish in "reeducation camps." A fly would be mistaken if it thought that the communist Spider would nominate worthy bishops. Cardinal Zen, just a few years short of his ninetieth birthday, has made two arduous and futile trips to Rome, hoping to staunch this diplomatic wound. Redolent of Mindszenty, he has said: "Pope Francis does not know the real Communist Party in China." Of Cardinal Parolin, the secretary of state who signed the agreement, he told a reporter: "I told the pope that he has a poisoned mind. He is very sweet, but I have no trust in this person. He believes in diplomacy, but not in our faith."

Pope Francis agreed to recognize the legitimacy of seven Communist-approved bishops, previously excommunicated, while removing two bishops loyal to Rome. Since the signing of the Vatican-China pact, a bishop appointed by the Vatican has been arrested by the Communist government and placed in a "reeducation camp" with no comment from the Vatican. This was Bishop Zhumin's fifth arrest in two years. Two government-sponsored bishops, one of whom was excommunicated by Pope Benedict in 2010, were welcome guests at this year's Synod on Youth. [9] One month after the diplomatic pact, the Chinese government contemptuously destroyed two Catholic shrines in the provinces of Shanxi and

[9]   Courtney Mares, "Tiananmen Square to St. Peter's Square: Who Are the Chinese Bishops at the Synod?," Catholic News Agency, October 17, 2018, https://www.catholicnewsagency.com/news/tiananmen-square-to-st-peters-who-are-the-chinese-bishops-at-the-synod-75699.

Guizhou. Uncertain is the fate of thirty bishops of the "Underground Church" loyal to the Holy See. Cardinal Zen laments the "annihilation" of the Catholic Church in China. State supervision of the Catholic Church has been placed under the total control of the Chinese Communist Party by a directive of Xi Jinping who, having abolished limits to his term of office, is a virtual dictator of the entire country. He has forbidden prayers, catechesis, and preaching to be published online.

Meanwhile, Bishop Marcelo Sanchez Sorondo, chancellor of the Pontifical Academy of Social Sciences, has hailed Communist China as the world's best exemplar of Catholic social teaching and called it a "land of wonders." Fr. Bernardo Cervellera, editor of *AsiaNews*, responded: "The idolization of China is an ideological affirmation that makes a laughingstock of the Church and harms the world." There is a fourteenth-century maxim that warns: "He who sups with the Devil should have a long spoon." The Vatican might need to change its spoon to chopsticks. Cardinal Zen offers more edifying counsel to his persecuted Catholic flock: "They take away your churches? You can no longer officiate? Go home, and pray with your family. Till the soil. Wait for better times. Go back to the catacombs. Communism isn't eternal."

Groundwork for the recent Vatican-China accord was laid by ex-cardinal Theodore McCarrick. He made at least eight trips to China over twenty years, advocating closer ties with President Xi Jinping. While privately inhibited by Pope Benedict XVI, who also canceled negotiations with Communist China, McCarrick was rehabilitated by Pope Francis, in whose election he claimed to have been a protagonist, after which he was sent on another mission to China. In an interview in 2016 for a semi-official journal of the Chinese government, the *Global Times*, McCarrick said that similarities between Pope Francis and Xi Jinping could be "a special gift for the world." He explained: "A lot of things that China worries

A Nursery Rhyme Pope Francis Would Do Well to Read

about, [Pope Francis] worries about: about the care of poor, older people, children, our civilization and especially the ecology." It is true that Pope Francis has frequently expressed more affinity for socialism than for capitalism. During his trip to Bolivia in 2015, he somewhat anachronistically invoked the fourth-century saint Basil of Caesarea to condemn "corporations, loan agencies, and certain free trade treaties." Indulging his propensity for coprological metaphors, the pope called capitalist profits the "dung of the Devil."

Of the twelve apostles, only one was a diplomat, and he is the only one of them who was not a saint, having drunk a toxic cocktail of arrogance and naïveté. This recipe is still fatal. Mary Howitt, moral dissector of "The Spider and the Fly," had reason in her generation for devotion "to the pope and not the papacy." In the ticking hours of our generation, there may be some cause for reversing this. It is a matter too grave to be tossed about lightly in a mere essay, but there is wise counsel in the ending of her poem:

And now, dear little children, who may this story read,
To idle, silly, flattering words, I pray you ne'er give heed:
Unto an evil counsellor close heart, and ear, and eye,
And take a lesson from this tale of the Spider and the Fly.

November 27, 2018

Music for the Holy Souls

The biographies of classical composers could give the impression that irregular behavior has been almost a necessary attribute of great talent. A particularly rank example is the uniquely inventive Renaissance composer of sacred music and madrigals, Carlo Gesualdo, prince of Venosa, who murdered his wife and her lover, mutilated their corpses, and exposed them naked in the town square. He was a nephew of St. Carlo Borromeo. Beethoven was notorious for his domestic squalor and explosive temper, and Handel could fly off the handle at the sound of an ill-tuned cello. Purcell and Sibelius spent more time in taverns than in concert halls. The cleric Vivaldi was banned from Verona to protect its schoolgirls, and Bruckner later indulged a similar attraction, along with a fascination with human skulls.

Wagner could not abide rooms with forty-five-degree corners and insisted that they be hung with yellow perfumed silk. His cult of Nordic racism set a bad precedent. Many of his original scores were destroyed along with Hitler in the Berlin bunker, and to this day his operas are not performed in Israel. Scriabin was of a different outlook, being a theosophist devotee of Madame Blavatsky. Schoenberg so suffered from triskaidekaphobia that he hid under his bedcovers on the thirteenth day of each month, unlike Wagner, who thought the number could augur good as well as evil. Satie owned one hundred umbrellas and two grand pianos, which he stacked one on top of the other. Mahler was so absentminded that he would stir his coffee with a cigarette.

On the other hand, Bach kept a happy household crammed with twenty children, plus many students, and was the trusty object of their affection. No one had a bad word for kindly "Papa" Haydn: a cheerful soul who prayed the Rosary for musical inspiration. If one didn't mind Mozart's sophomoric humor and what some scholars think may have been Tourette syndrome, he was by all accounts a genial companion, as was Mendelssohn, notwithstanding those infrequent fits when he would berate German relatives in an incoherent form of English. George Gershwin had a normal boyhood, playing stickball on the streets of Brooklyn until his parents bought a piano. And then there is the almost abnormal normalcy of the self-taught composer Sir Edward Elgar (1857–1934).

He was born in a placid English village outside Worcester and cultivated an unaffected benignity that made him countless friends. William, his father, was a piano tuner, owned a sheet music shop, and played the violin well enough to perform in the Three Choirs Festival in Worcester. His mother Ann was the ample and amiable daughter of a farmer. Edward was the fourth of her seven children, whom she reared in the Catholicism to which she had converted. William disapproved of this, but only mildly since he was the paid organist in the Jesuit Church of St. George in Worcester. His son would succeed him there. Today, the renovated organ still has the stops used by Edward, marked with an "E." The handsome church, which now belongs to the archdiocese of Birmingham, has over the altar a large reproduction of Raphael's Transfiguration, a gift in 1837 from the sixteenth Earl of Shrewsbury, John Talbot. The Catholic "Good Earl John" was revered for his munificence to the Church. The original Raphael work had been commissioned in 1517 by Cardinal Giulio de' Medici who, before becoming Pope Clement VII, had been titular bishop of Worcester.

As a young piano teacher, Elgar proposed marriage to his student Alice Roberts, who was fluent in five languages and eventually became a proficient author of poetry and novels. She was born in Gujarat, India, where her father was a major-general. Her family did not approve of a marriage beneath her station, especially not to a Catholic since Alice's great-grandfather, Robert Raikes, had founded the Sunday School system in the Church of England. The couple wed in London's Brompton Oratory.

Alice proved to be a mainstay in periods when her husband seemed unnoticed or even discouraged. Once when he was idly playing a few notes on the piano, she said, "That's a pretty tune, Eddie—keep it." And so issued forth "Nimrod," the ninth of the *Enigma Variations*. Each is a musical sketch of one of Elgar's unnamed friends. In the Old Testament, Noah's great-grandson was Nimrod, the "great hunter." So this ninth section was meant for the composer's advocate at the Novello publishing house, Augustus Jaeger, whose name means "hunter" in German. This variation's haunting solemnity has made it a set piece for countless memorial services and commemorations. It is played each Remembrance Day at the Cenotaph on Whitehall in the presence of the sovereign. A choral setting of it uses a text from the Requiem Mass:

> Lux aeterna luceat eis, Domine,
> Cum sanctis tuis in aeternum,
> Quia pius es.
> Requiem aeternam dona eis, Domine,
> Et lux perpetua luceat eis.

> "May light eternal shine upon them, O Lord,
> With Thy saints forever,
> For Thou art Kind.
> Eternal rest give to them, O Lord,
> And let perpetual light shine upon them."

Our Peculiar Times

In 1900, two years after the *Enigma Variations*, Elgar set to music Cardinal Newman's long poem, *The Dream of Gerontius*. Elgar thought of it as a unique form and resisted calling it an "oratorio," even though such had sound ecclesiastical credentials from the days of the Oratory of St. Philip Neri. It is about the deathbed struggle of a man trying to prepare his soul for the eternal habitations. Alice had given a copy of Newman's poem to Edward as a wedding present ("'til death do us part") and Dvorak had personally discussed with Newman the possibility of setting it to music. Parts of the text are, or should be, familiar hymns that justly occlude some of the banalities that pass today for funeral music, with corpses flying off on "Eagle's Wings." There are, for instance, "Firmly I Believe, and Truly," and the mighty "Praise to the Holiest in the Height," which had already become popular hymns with different tunes.

Elgar and the Viennese violinist Fritz Kreisler greatly admired each other, and in 1910 Kreisler commissioned a violin concerto from him. After a chance encounter in New York in 1947, Msgr. Fulton Sheen, then a professor of philosophy at the Catholic University of America, instructed Kreisler and his wife and regularized their marriage. Sheen claimed them as converts, although this was not quite accurate since Kreisler, though of Jewish ancestry, had long before been baptized. But Sheen visited them regularly and preached at their funerals.

Elgar stopped composing after his wife died in 1920. At her funeral, a quartet of his surviving friends played the Andante section of his String Quartet in E Minor, composed after so many of his other friends had not survived the Great War. Edward and Alice are buried next to their daughter in the churchyard of St. Wulstan's in Little Malvern, which now is in the care of the Benedictines of Downside Abbey.

Although Elgar considered *Gerontius* to be his masterpiece, the first of Elgar's *Coronation Marches* is surely his best-known work, and rare has been a college graduation ceremony without it. Having written the marches in honor of Edward VII, Elgar himself became a symbol of the sturdiest heights of Edwardiana, and he physically resembled that other symbol of the age, Rudyard Kipling; their lives were virtually coterminous. The words for the "Land of Hope and Glory" March were written by Arthur Benson, brother of the convert preacher and author Msgr. Robert Hugh Benson. Elgar did not thirst for honors, but was not unsatisfied when George V made him a baronet and "Master of the King's Musick."

Performances of Elgar's *Gerontius* were banned in the Anglican cathedrals of Gloucester and Peterborough because of its Catholic theology of Purgatory. Hubert Parry appreciated the acoustics when he heard it for the first time in the yet unfinished Westminster Cathedral, but he sniffed: "It reeks too much of the morbid and unnatural terrors and hysterics engendered by priestcraft to be congenial — vivid though it certainly is."

Gerontius means "old man" and represents Everyman, and the doctrines of particular judgment, Purgatory, and the intercession of the saints are blessings of God's grace for mortal souls. In these wistful autumnal days when the liturgical commemorations of All Saints and All Souls set the theme, the melody of "Nimrod" and the lines of *Gerontius* give a confused world a dose of reality. They are a sturdy relief from the depressing attempts of a secular culture to "celebrate life" artificially at funerals when in fact such awkwardness harbors a pagan fear of death. But as Newman wrote and Elgar played:

> Now that the hour is come, my fear is fled;
> And at this balance of my destiny,
> Now close upon me, I can forward look
> With a serenest joy.

October 31, 2018

The Morality of Tattooing

There was a time, not in the hoary past, when tattoos were an indulgence of louche members of the demimonde, as observed by Alexandre Dumas. They seem to have become respectable as our culture erases the borderline between the demimonde and the *monde entier*. Priests have become somewhat accustomed to pious communicants with arms totally decorated like a Persian tapestry or Michelin roadmap, in what is idiomatically called a "sleeve." Even facial tattoos are appearing. Some are in the form of written slogans, which one supposes would appear to a narcissist backward in a mirror. Other designs are more audacious, such as the portrait of Anne Frank on the cheek of the "hip-hop" producer Arnold Gutierrez. One used to have to go to state fair sideshows to see tattooed men like those who have become part of the vernacular on Main Street. Roughly over one-fifth of all adults in the United States now sport more than one tattoo, up from about 14 percent in 2003, although these figures are, of course, estimates.

One practical problem with this fad — if it is just a fad — is that, unlike hairstyles or clothing, it cannot be corrected in mature years. If these markings can be removed, it is only by a long and painful process, more so if the depiction is in a less accessible part of the body. But the bigger issue is whether a tattoo befits what is increasingly referred to with unqualified insouciance as "the dignity of the human person." If it is undignified to execute someone, whatever the crime may be, as some would now propose, is it unworthy to turn the human body into a human billboard? And if the body is a temple of the Holy Spirit (1 Cor. 6:19–20), are such decorations embellishments or defacements?

An Old Testament prohibition of what was considered a pagan practice (Lev. 19:28) was for a particular time and circumstance, and not all Levitical prohibitions have universal application for the Christian. Yet the Council of Northumberland in England decreed in 787, the same year as the Second Council of Nicaea: "When an individual undergoes the ordeal of tattooing for the sake of God, he is greatly praised. But one who submits himself to be tattooed for superstitious reason in the manner of the heathens will derive no benefit thereof."

A possible forgery paraded an outright prohibition of tattooing as a pontifical decree of Adrian I, but there was a logic to it. Pope Adrian had aligned himself with the Franks against the tattooed Lombards who were nibbling at papal territories, the final straw being the boldness of the Lombard king Desiderius in seizing the Duchy of the Pentapolis. The problem was solved soon enough, during the reigns of Cunincpert and Liutprand, when the Lombards became totally Catholicized. (In one of those curious circumstances that may be less significant than one might wish, the largest tattoo parlor in Portland, Oregon, in our own time is on Lombard Street.) Before Adrian, in the fourth century, St. Basil the Great had declared: "No man shall let his hair grow long or tattoo himself as do the heathen, those apostles of Satan who make themselves despicable by indulging in lewd and lascivious thought. Do not associate with those who mark themselves with thorns and needles so that their blood flows to the earth."

In 316, the practice of tattooing the faces of criminals was abolished as un-Christian by the emperor Constantine. In part this may have been because "followers of the Chrestus" had been so branded. In addition, the Romans had been perplexed, and admittedly terrified, by the Picts, who painted themselves in dark indigo from head to toe. They were an enigmatic people who eventually intermarried with clans from the Inner Hebrides and contiguous parts. Their society was partly matriarchal, and the women were even more "depicted" than their men. It is not certain if they really were tattooed, or just wore war paint like the American Indians, but it is certain that they used a dye from the "woad" plant, a form of mustard, which, even if injected beneath the skin, would last only a couple of weeks.

There is evidence that, before the Edict of Milan, many Christians deliberately tattooed themselves in bold defiance, rather like the unsubstantiated report of King Christian X's wearing a yellow Star of David during the Nazi occupation of Denmark. Later, Christian tattoos proclaimed the Faith in the Holy Land and Anatolia, as recorded by Procopius of Gaza in the sixth century and a century later by Theophylact Simocatta. For some, tattoos replicated the wounds of Christ. Crusaders customarily had themselves tattooed to identify their bodies as Christian for burial. During Ottoman rule in Bosnia, Christian Croats used tattoos to prevent conversions to Islam. Tattooing the right wrist with an image of the Cross is still common among Copts; the Gerges family ply their tattooing trade at the Church of St. Simon the Tanner in the Mokattam hills.

Tattoos go back even further: there are tattoos on the five-thousand-year-old body of the Ice Man (Oetzi) found frozen in the Alps. Their purposes are unknown, and at least in part were probably a kind of talisman. There is a greater frequency of tattooing among the mentally ill today, but many psychiatrists think that their use by relatively normal people is often a passive-aggressive way of compensating for low self-esteem, especially among young adults.

Our Peculiar Times

This is even more so the case in extreme forms of body piercing. A Mayo Clinic report has drawn attention to the increased risk of infections such as Hepatitis B and C through the use of tattoo needles.

First Tattooed American

John Ledyard, a Dartmouth College undergraduate who matriculated in 1772, later became the first American tattooed in the Polynesian manner, and saw nothing inconsistent in this and his Christian zeal, influenced by the First Great Awakening. While proficient in Greek and Latin and skilled in classical drama, he was unable to pay his tuition, and left the college in a dugout canoe, rowing down the Connecticut River to New London. Robert Frost would call him "the patron saint of freshman dropouts." Then he sailed to England, where he joined the crew of Captain Cook on his third journey aboard the HMS *Resolution* in search of the Northwest Passage. He served as a mariner, with the master being William Bligh, who was later to attain opprobrium as captain of the HMS *Bounty*. In Polynesia, Ledyard's arms and hands were tattooed with reddish brown dots in a geometric pattern. It was Cook who adopted the Polynesian name "ta-tau." This is not to be confused with the seventeenth-century Dutch drumbeat "doe den tap toe" signifying closing hour for drinking in barracks, from which we get the military tattoo, such as the Royal Edinburgh Tattoo.

The American naval historian Ira Dye debunked the belief that Captain Cook was the first to introduce a Polynesian style of tattooing to the West, having had his buttocks tattooed in Tahiti. Various explorers were already familiar with the practice, and in 1791 the remarkable hydrographer and explorer Charles Pierre Claret de Fleurieu, who barely escaped the guillotine, remarked a similarity with practices long established in Europe.

The Morality of Tattooing

After being the first U.S. citizen to see Alaska, Ledyard returned briefly to Dartmouth and wrote a journal of Captain Cook's last expedition to the Sandwich Islands and beyond, including an account of his death at the hands of Hawaiians in Kealakekua Bay. This was the first book to receive a copyright in the new nation of the United States. Ledyard then embarked for Paris, where he was befriended by John Paul Jones and Benjamin Franklin. Thomas Jefferson, as minister to the court of Louis XVI, introduced him as the first tattooed American at Versailles and secured him a passport from the empress Catherine the Great, hoping that Ledyard might cross Russia and secure a trade agreement with China. Agents of the empress arrested him in the Siberian town of Irkutsk as a possible spy and deported him to Poland. He eventually ended up in Egypt, seeking the source of the Niger River, and died in Cairo of accidental poisoning at the age of thirty-seven.

It cannot be said that tattooing became acceptable among Ledyard's fellow Connecticut Yankees, but eventually it attained a sort of esoteric caché among European aristocrats, and not without precedent. King Harold II had tattoos of his various victories illustrated all over his body, but certainly not the Battle of Hastings. In 1862, as Prince of Wales, the future Edward VII received the first of several tattoos, a Jerusalem cross, while in the Holy Land. His son George V, while Duke of York, was tattooed with a dragon on his arm in 1882 during his trip to Japan, and suit was followed by the rulers of Spain, Denmark, and Germany. Winston's mother, Lady Randolph Churchill, had a snake tattooed on her wrist, and her son copied her with an anchor like Popeye's on his arm.

Maori Culture Down Under

Nowhere is tattooing so artistically developed as among the Maori of New Zealand, probably through Samoan influences. But the

Our Peculiar Times

Maori method is unique and different from generic tattooing. "Ta moko" involves incising the skin, leaving a grooved surface. While this came to be considered barbaric among some Pacific populations, being totally abolished in late nineteenth-century Japan, *ta moko* lasted for a while as a Maori status symbol, although Catholic missionaries discouraged it. In order to combat smallpox with modern medicine, the Tohunga Suppression Act of 1907 restricted the incantatory rites of tattooed *tohunga*, or medicine men, a stricture made absolute by the Quackery Prevention Act of 1908 during the reign of the admittedly tattooed Edward VII.

No one is more symbolic of the modern Maori identity and cultural pride than Whina Cooper (1895–1994). The granddaughter of an American whaler and daughter of Catholic catechist Heremia Te Wake, Cooper was born in northern Hokianga, where unsung heroic missionaries had arrived in 1838, bringing the gospel to the Ngāpuhi region despite many obstacles and dangers. In her long life, from simple beginnings, she championed Maori property rights, leading the famous Maori Land March of 1975 from Te Hāpua to Wellington. In her marriage, which contravened tribal customs, she was protected and mentored by a priest, Fr. Charles Kreymborg.

In 1981, Queen Elizabeth II honored Cooper as a Dame of the Order of the British Empire. By her life's end, she was popularly called "Mother of the Nation" and a million people watched her funeral on television. In recent times, Nanaia Mahuta became the first member of the New Zealand Parliament to wear a *moko kauae*, reviving the traditional chin tattoo worn by distinguished women, but Dame Whina, not particularly opinionated about the matter, had managed to do more than any other Maori woman without it.

There has been something of a resurgence of *ta moko* as a cultural statement. The Maori have a traditional welcoming ceremony for strangers, and I had the honor of participating in one in Auckland. They affect a ferocity completely out of character with their kindly character, for it is sheer theater. Tattooed warriors wear abbreviated clothing suitable for tropical heat and perform a ritual dance, the *haka*, meant to intimidate the visitor with its menacing sounds, grimacing faces, and threatening gestures. If one does not blink, one is welcome. I passed the test easily, since I travel frequently on the New York City subway system.

Amputating the Expressive Possibilities

To bring this into the current Western cultural sphere, a committee report of the Pontifical Council for Culture in Rome on January 29, 2015, addressed the question of cosmetic alteration of the human body, and disapproved of procedures such as "facelifts" and "tummy tucks," pronouncing that elective plastic surgery can "amputate the expressive possibilities of the human face which are so connected to empathetic abilities" and "can be aggressive toward the feminine identity, showing a refusal of the body." Something may have been lost in the received text as rendered by Vatican translators under the innocent impression that they have a capacity for English, but one infers that the commission would not approve of tattoos.

However, in Rome's Palazzo Colonna in February 2018, at a "sneak preview" of the Metropolitan Museum of Art's controversial *Heavenly Bodies* exhibition, which opened in New York the following May, Cardinal Gianfranco Ravasi, president of the Pontifical Council for Culture, was photographed smiling next to the fashion designer Donatella Versace, who could not smile because surgical procedures had limited her expressive possibilities. Ravasi was the same prelate who keened in 2016 at news of the death of David Bowie, the singer whose left calf was tattooed with an image of a man on a bicycle holding a frog.

At a gathering of three hundred young adults in Rome on May 19, 2018, a seminarian from Ukraine, where a tattoo festival is held annually in Kyiv, asked Pope Francis for a pontifical opinion on tattooing. In a development of the imputed anti-tattoo doctrine of Pope Adrian I, while supposedly not contradicting it, His Holiness said, "Don't be afraid of tattoos," and cited the example of Eritrean Christians tattooed with crosses. He added: "Of course, there can be exaggerations," but a tattoo "is a sign of belonging" and talking about it can begin "a dialogue about priorities."

Perhaps in a less spontaneous encounter, the Holy Father might have added that the Holy Catholic Church provides three sacraments whose character is more indelible than any self-mutilation. Baptism, Confirmation, and Holy Orders cannot be repeated, and confer a seal by which one belongs to Christ and is disposed to actual graces. This is the message that missionaries spread throughout the world, and that needs to be heard again in the homelands of those missionaries.

August 23, 2018

A Woman of Science: Maria Gaetana Agnesi

A cavalcade of women whose scientific achievements have had an important impact on the way we live and do things challenges any attempt to stereotype these geniuses as colorless drones or "nerds," which is merely a neologism of Dr. Seuss from 1950. For instance, the mathematician Gabrielle Émilie Le Tonnelier de Breteuil was an elegant if wayward mistress of Voltaire and also had a child by a minor poet, the Marquis de Saint-Lambert, while sustaining the affection of her long-suffering husband, the Marquis du Châtelet-Lomont. In 1749, she died at the age of forty-three, having given birth to a short-lived girl at her desk while translating some of Newton's *Principia*. The newborn was placed on a large leather-bound volume illustrating infinitesimal calculus. A generation earlier, the German entomologist Maria Merian raised eyebrows when she outfitted herself for a dangerous journey to study insects in Suriname.

In England, the paleontologist Mary Anning, impoverished daughter of a cabinetmaker who died when she was eleven, spent much of her life searching for late-Jurassic fossils in the cliffs at Lyme Regis and was rewarded with the first discovery of what she named an ichthyosaurus, before she died in 1847, one year before the death of Caroline Herschel. Caroline was German and was told by her father that she was too ungainly to attract a husband.

Eventually, she left her work as a housekeeper to assist her brother in England with his musical and astronomical interests. She polished the telescope with which he discovered the planet Uranus, took up the science herself, and discovered eight comets. Laden with pensions from British royals and the king of Prussia, she was still observing the stars when she died at age ninety-six.

Augusta Ada King-Noel, the Countess of Lovelace, was no less exotic than her father, Lord Byron, but the principal influence on her talents was her tutor, the astronomer Mary Somerville, for whom the college in Oxford is named. Ada was only thirty-six at her death in 1852, but packed a lot into those years, and, having invented the first algorithm for a mechanical computer called the "Analytical Engine," she has claim to being the first computer programmer.

The entombment of Marie Skłodowska Curie in the Pantheon in Paris in 1995 was sixty-one years after her death from aplastic anemia, the result of her immeasurably beneficial work as the discoverer of radium and polonium. As a naturalized French citizen, she was the devoted wife of Pierre, whose death when run over by a carriage left her widowed with two small children. Her favorite cookbook is preserved, but remains too radioactive to be handled. Her daughter Irène discovered artificial radioactivity, and died at the age of fifty-eight, stricken with leukemia. Thus both of them were martyrs of science, and are the only mother-daughter Nobel laureates.

These names in various ways inspired the inventiveness of countless more recent figures. Having come to the United States and settled in Bryn Mawr upon her expulsion by the Nazis, Emmy Noether (d. 1935) established her reputation as the preeminent abstract algebraist of her generation. The granddaughter of Madame Curie, Hélène Langevin-Joliot, is a nuclear physicist, still active at the age of ninety-one in 2018. Attaining a medical degree at Johns

Hopkins in 1920, Helen Taussig saved the lives of thousands of infants as the founder of pediatric cardiology, which she managed to do despite her dyslexia and deafness. Her motto was "Learn to listen with your fingers." When Rosalind Franklin died in 1958, she had laid the groundwork for Watson and Crick's discovery of DNA. Lisa Meitner (d. 1968), an Austrian who, as a Jew, fled the Nazis, discovered nuclear fission; Barbara McClintock's Nobel Prize in physiology before her death in 1992 was for her work as a cytogeneticist; and Dorothy Hodgkin (d. 1994), an Englishwoman born in Egypt, determined the structures of penicillin, insulin, and vitamin B12. One of her students in Oxford, the future prime minister Margaret Thatcher, kept her photograph in 10 Downing Street. Thatcher's university dissertation was on X-ray crystallography of the antibiotic cocktail gramicidin. Before entering politics, Thatcher worked as an industrial chemist at British Xylonite Plastics. While she regretted not having studied law, her radioactivity research at least metaphorically helped her to see through her opponents.

It belabors the obvious to remark that all of these scientists seem to have been happy in themselves, and would disdain the Gnostic polemics of the "transgender" lobby that pretends sexual identity is not a fact but a persuasion. Some of them reasonably complained about the way their femaleness was an obstacle in the eyes of some men. Just think of Mary Anning, denied membership to the Geological Society of London, although she could surpass in achievement all its self-satisfied male members: "The world has used me so unkindly, I fear it has made me suspicious of everyone." The Marquise du Châtelet had written an essay on how women had been impeded in scientific pursuits by the lack of secondary education. But unthinking prejudice has had a long history. For sore wounds in the annals of science, we can look back to the fifth century when fanatical Christian monks in Alexandria, possibly enflamed by the rhetoric of St. Cyril, dismembered the Neoplatonist philosopher, astronomer, and mathematician Hypatia.

The purpose of this essay is not to indulge in identity politics, and I mention this only as an aside. If discrimination against women in science has been a neuralgic matter, it was real nonetheless. After all, while there are lists of "famous female scientists," there is no instinct to compile lists of "famous male scientists." There is enough evidence to confound any imputation of lesser intelligence to women, but there have been periods when exceptionally bright women were called witches, while clever men were never called warlocks — save perhaps rarities like the polymath Gerbert of Aurillac after he became Pope Sylvester II — but that was only for political reasons. I can make only a domestic reference: my father was something of an inventor and engineering genius, a gift he did not pass on to me, but my mother could match him. She was a licensed volunteer Red Cross ambulance driver and auto mechanic during World War II, successful enough in her vigilance that the Nazis never invaded New Jersey, and she could fix a flat tire faster than I. In the heyday of Amelia Earhart, she took flying lessons in a craft that looked held together with string, and enjoyed the thrill of flying through turbulence, another gift not passed along to me. My parents were parted by death only briefly, and that symbiotic companionship is the nurse of the most benevolent science.

In 2014, an Iranian mathematician at Stanford University, Maryam Mirzakhani, became the first woman to receive the highest of honors in her science, the Fields Medal, dying of breast cancer three years later at age forty. It remains that only 9 percent of all editors of mathematics journals are women, and women hold only 15 percent of the tenure-track positions in mathematics, 14 percent in engineering, and 18 percent in computer science. Yet women match men in the number of undergraduate degrees in science, and we know from experience that they generally have a higher verbal competence that only hearing-impaired men could deny, and score higher on most science tests. The scholastic attribution of inductivity to men and intuitiveness to women is a useful distinction, though always wrong when applied absolutely. It allows us to see a complementarity between male and female personalities in scientific research. There is also the consideration that many women have maternal obligations, which rightly have priority, but the maternal instinct also explains why women in general, avoiding the danger of overstatement, have a greater affinity for sciences involving living things rather than things inanimate. It may be significant that they shine in obstetrics and comprise 75 percent of all veterinary doctors. There is evidence this difference in interest manifests itself in other professions and helps explain sex inequalities by occupation.

All this sows enough seeds for discussion, and is tangential to the Catholic lady who pursued a scientific career bonded with a mystical contemplation of Christ's Death and Resurrection that animated her whole life. Maria Gaetana Agnesi was the first woman to attain worldwide fame as a mathematician. She followed the first woman to receive a doctorate in philosophy, Elena Piscopia (1646–1684). A Venetian, Piscopia spoke seven languages by the age of ten and, as a Benedictine oblate, dedicated her advanced musical talents and erudition in mathematics and astronomy to the Lord who had given her brains and everything else. The second European to become a doctor of philosophy, and the first to hold a university chair in physics, was the Bolognese physicist Laura Bassi (1711–1778). She worked closely with her husband in electrical experimentation, studying the work of Benjamin Franklin, while birthing twelve children.

When Archbishop Lambertini became Pope Benedict XIV, having been her patron in Bologna, he fought opposition to make her one of the twenty-five members of his scientific academy. She is buried in Bologna in the Church of Corpus Domini next to Luigi Galvani, father of bioelectromagnetics, in whose honor "galvanizing" is named. If explorers ever make it to the planet Venus, they will find a crater named for Professor Bassi, along with one for Maria Agnesi. Bassi was roughly contemporary with Agnesi, who was seven years her junior. Agnesi was born exactly three hundred years ago, in the year that the French mathematician Jacques Ozanam died. As a devout Catholic, he would probably not mind that his legacy is eclipsed by his great-grandnephew, Frédéric Ozanam, who founded the Society of St. Vincent de Paul.

Maria Agnesi's father, who was a professor of mathematics in Milan, encouraged his daughter in the basic liberal arts as well as classical and modern languages, and she proved a polyglot like Elena Piscopia under the tutelage of a priest who was her cousin. From an early age her studies included serious theology, for her thwarted ambition was to be a nun. Her father, prosperous himself but desirous of an aristocratic connection, married into Milanese nobility, but when his wife died, he wed twice more, with eventually twenty-one children. Maria as the eldest was responsible for their care. Shy by nature, she nevertheless obliged her proud father by giving lectures in Latin, one of them a discourse on the importance of educating women, to his fellow professors. Her major mathematical work was a two-volume text on differential and integral calculus, and she also advanced the study of conical sections.

Pope Benedict XIV had her appointed to a full professorship of mathematics and natural philosophy in his beloved university of Bologna, an honorific which she accepted but never exercised. Although most attractive and propertied, she never married, and the death of her father in 1752 freed her to devote the last forty years of her life to prayer and study of the Early Fathers. Her most significant work on the role of reason in mystical contemplation was *Il cielo mistico*. She testified: "Man always acts to achieve goals;

A Woman of Science: Maria Gaetana Agnesi

the goal of the Christian is the glory of God. I hope my studies have brought glory to God, as they were useful to others, and derived from obedience, because that was my father's will. Now I have found better ways and means to serve God, and to be useful to others."

Those decades enabled her to form the Pio Albergo Trivulzio for care of the sick poor, and she turned her house into an infirmary and hospice where she personally nursed the afflicted and comforted the dying. To provide for this, she sold her own lands and belongings, including diamonds given her by the empress Maria Theresa, and gold prizes awarded by Pope Benedict. Her body was interred in an unmarked grave with fifteen paupers.

The prodigy's sister, Maria Teresa Agnesi Pinottini, was a composer, harpsichordist, singer, and librettist, and on occasion accompanied her sibling's lectures with incidental music. She composed seven operas, as well as various arias for the empress to sing in Vienna. Her portrait hangs at La Scala. Recently, the Sonoma winery of Francis Ford Coppola has bottled an "Agnesi 1799" brandy in honor of the mathematician, along with a gin named for the astronomer Ada Lovelace.

This tercentenary year of the birth of Maria Gaetana Agnesi should be a celebration. In our age of rapid canonizations, it is well to remember that she left this world over two centuries ago, and a cause in her name might be neither hasty nor remiss. Words of Jacques Ozanam certainly would be a fine epitaph for her: "It is for doctors to dispute, for the pope to decide, and for mathematicians to go to heaven in a perpendicular line."

August 14, 2018

Bare-Knuckle Religion

The recent pardon of the late world heavyweight champion Jack
Johnson by our president was a gracious act long overdue. A previous motion had passed the House but died in the Senate in 2008.
Johnson's racially motivated conviction for violating the Mann
Act after he had married a white woman resulted in his beginning
a year term in Leavenworth prison in 1920. It was not a salutary
place; I buried one of its inmates who had done much more than a
year there. Johnson skipped bail and spent several years in Europe
via Canada. In Barcelona, much in need of funds that had run
out, although he had garnered fantastic box-office fees in illegal
matches and had squandered them with commensurate prodigality,
he undertook an exhibition match while on the lam in 1916. The
site was a bullring near the church of Sagrada Familia. Johnson's
opponent was Arthur Cravan, a Swiss amateur boxer and Dadaist
poet also in need of funds. The match was brief, as Cravan froze at
the sight of the "Galveston Giant." They fought by the eponymous
rules of the Marquis of Queensberry, first published in 1867. As one
of those curiosities only to be sorted out in the eternal habitations,
the Marquess had brought the legal action leading to the downfall
of Oscar Wilde, who was Cravan's uncle. The atheist Marquess
died ten months before Wilde, and both were received into the
Catholic Church on their deathbeds.

Our Peculiar Times

In Johnson's early days, all professional boxing was illegal in the United States. His "Fight of the Century" against James Jeffries in 1910, spectacularly captured on film, earned him over $1.7 million in today's money, but it also caused a race riot. Because of the sullen unrest, Theodore Roosevelt urged that the film be censored: "The last contest provoked a very unfortunate display of race antagonism.... It would be an admirable thing if some method could be devised to stop the exhibition of the moving pictures taken thereof." But Johnson's success was a bit like Jesse Owens's moral triumph at the Berlin Olympics. Before that, in 1889, the monumental bout of John L. Sullivan (who quickly left Boston College, where his Irish immigrant parents had placed him in hopes that he would become a priest) was fought against Jake Kilrain. Six state governors cooperated to see that the fight would take place with the law looking the other way. Hard to believe, the fight lasted seventy rounds with bare knuckles, on a farm in Richburg, Mississippi, before a crowd of three thousand in temperatures above one hundred degrees, and the canvas was not innocent of blood. It took two hours and eighteen minutes. This still does not surpass the longest bare-knuckle fight at six hours and fifteen minutes between James Kelly and Jonathan Smith in Victoria, Australia, in 1855. Sullivan was befriended by Theodore Roosevelt, whom he coached. The president continued to spar in the White House until a young artillery officer permanently blinded Roosevelt in one eye after a blow detached the retina of the fifty-year-old chief executive. This was never disclosed to the public.

In 1945, raising money for war bonds, Jack Johnson managed to fight an exhibition match in New York City at the age of sixty-seven, consisting in three one-minute rounds each against Joe Jeanette and John Ballcourt. Exactly two years later, to the very month in the same Madison Square Garden, the disreputable fight manager Frank "Blinky" Palermo fixed the Jake LaMotta–Billy

Fox fight. He is not to be confused with Servant of God Joseph of Palermo, who before becoming a Capuchin had been expelled from several schools for punching some of his classmates. He is invoked as a patron of boxers and those with bad tempers, although the more commonly cited patron is St. Nicholas of Myra because, perhaps with some embellishment of the narrative, he is said to have punched the heretic Arius at the Council of Nicaea in 325. *Sancte Nicolae percute pro nobis.*

The original Queensberry rules required gloves, but did not specify their weight. In early days they averaged just two ounces, compared with ten-to-twelve ounces today. Some maintain that boxing gloves can inflict more harm because of more sustained punching, but forensic computer calculations estimate that bare-knuckle fights have roughly fourteen thousand traumatic injuries per million blows measured against seventy-six per million with gloves.

If there is a sweetness in having one's predictions vindicated, it is a bitter sweetness when the result is not good. So, for instance, I predicted in a volume published in 1971, when the ordination of women was only something of an academic speculation, that its character as a Gnostic misunderstanding would logically lead to attempts at marriage between the same sexes. At the time, this was ridiculed as some sort of absurd adynaton. My vindication is not happy because the result has been so sad. On a more banal level, I was criticized for warning in an article in *Crisis* in 2013 that legalization of mixed martial arts (MMA) would lead to worse coarseness.[10] Alas, the unblushing oracle in me was right. Bare-knuckle boxing, which was never sanctioned in the United States, became approved when Wyoming became the first to legalize it

[10] Fr. George W. Rutler, "The Christian Boxer," *Crisis Magazine*, April 8, 2013, https://www.crisismagazine.com/2013/the-christian-boxer.

on March 20 of this year at the behest of that state's MMA commission, 130 years after John L. Sullivan pranced in the ring. The first match was shown live on pay-per-view television on June 2, broadcast from the Ice & Events Center in Cheyenne, Wyoming. Bare-knuckle proponents claim that gloves were intended only to protect the hands, allowing the fighter to land more punches and throw harder, but the sanguinary scenes in Cheyenne disgraced the "sweet science" emblematic in the grace of fighters such as Gene Tunney and Joe Lewis and their ranks of confreres.

At the tournament in Cheyenne, Bobby Gunn and nineteen other pros went at it. Reggie Burnette bloodied Travis "the Animal" Thompson. According to the Associated Press: "Arnold Adams, a 32-year-old MMA heavyweight, pounded ex-UFC fighter D.J. Linderman's face into a bloody mess in front of 2,000 rowdy fans at a hockey rink that usually hosts birthday parties and skating lessons in Wyoming's capital." In the female division (at least femaleness is still considered an objective correlate) Bec Rawlings, a mother of two, attacked Alma Garcia in the second round on a technical knockout. The spectacle made female mud wrestling look like the Bolshoi Ballet.

I am not one to surrender boxing to the lesser sports, and I am on record as having participated ever so humbly in the ring myself. I helped to start what is now a biannual boxing exhibition match in my club in New York City, named for one of our former members, Teddy Roosevelt. I also know the importance of taping hands before putting gloves on, since one of my sparring partners fractured his fifth metacarpal, requiring surgery, because I had neglected to help tape his hand one inch up to the knuckles. But as some of my predictions in the past have been realized, I can anticipate that as our culture continues to devolve in ways beyond the worst fears of past pessimists, it is possible that legal bare-knuckle boxing will lead to other games more despoiling of human dignity. If infants can be aborted and the elderly smothered, how is it impossible that the bloodlust of crowds in stadiums who watch men and women smash faces with their knuckles will want to watch people stab each other and feed underlings to starved beasts as in days of old?

This, I grant, is possibly a theatric fear, but it is spoken with knowledge of colosseums where laureled civilizations thought that they had attained the apex of human achievement. In some respects the Roman Empire achieved greatly, but it also sported horribly. Their caesars included Lucius Aurelius Commodus, who imagined himself the reincarnation of Hercules, and entertained crowds by decapitating ostriches and killing cripples for entertainment. For any hyperbole, I apologize, but these people did exist and can exist again. The sadism of modern tyrants in the last century is proof enough of that. But another man also existed in conflicted Rome: the monk St. Telemachus. According to the historian Theodoret, he jumped over a barrier into the middle of a gladiatorial arena in 391, tried to separate two of the fighters, and shouted, "In the name of Jesus Christ, stop these wicked games!" The mob in the stands stoned him to death with the approval of the city prefect, but the emperor Honorius fell silent and then banned the gladiatorial spectacles. The last gladiator fought on January 1, 404.

June 11, 2018

When C. S. Lewis Befriended
a Living Catholic Saint

When Luigi Calabria, a shoemaker married to a housemaid, died in
Verona, Italy, in 1882, the youngest of his seven sons, nine-year-old
Giovanni, had to quit school and take a job as an apprentice. A
local parish priest, Don Pietro Scapini, privately tutored him for the
minor seminary, from which he took a leave to serve two years in
the army. During that time, he established a remarkable reputation
for edifying his fellow soldiers and converting some of them. Even
before ordination, he established a charitable institution for the
care of poor sick people and, as a parish priest, he founded the Poor
Servants of Divine Providence in 1907. The society grew, receiving
diocesan approval in 1932. The women's branch he started in 1910
would become a refuge for Jewish women during the Second World
War. To his own surprise, since he was a rather private person, his
order spread from Italy to Brazil, Argentina, Uruguay, India, Kenya,
Romania, and the Philippines.

With remarkable economy of time, he was a keen reader,
and in 1947 he came across a book translated as *Le lettere di
Berlicche* by a professor at the University of Milan, Alberto Castelli, who later became a titular archbishop as vice president for
the Pontifical Council of the Laity. Berlicche was Screwtape and

Malacoda served for Wormwood. The original, of course, had been published in 1943 as *The Screwtape Letters*, and Calabria was so taken with it that he sent a letter of appreciation to the author in England. Lacking English, he wrote it in the Latin with which he had become proficient since his juvenile tutorials with Don Pietro.

It is annoying how some assume and assert that C. S. Lewis responded in *lingua Latina* only because he had no Italian. As a teenager in Northern Ireland, Lewis had become enamored of Dante, beginning with the *Purgatorio*, which began his fascination with Italian, including the work of Petrarch. Having first learned French and Latin, Lewis was soon to embark on Greek and other tongues including his beloved Old Norse. He quotes Italian lines from the *Paradiso* in his *Letters to Malcolm*. As a youth studying a Latin atlas of Italy, he was attracted to the name of an Umbrian town called Narnia, and put it in his memory bank where years later it bore fruit. Fr. Calabria knew that Latin would be second nature to an Oxford don. The sermon at the opening of each academic term is preached in Latin in the University Church of St. Mary the Virgin, with its charming if incongruous Solomonic pillars.

Even the Book of Common Prayer had been translated twice into Latin in the seventeenth century for university use as *Liber Precum Publicarum*. In the United States in 2008, an Episcopal clergyman admirably translated the updated 1979 edition into Latin, but its sales apparently were sparse because of his denomination's demographic and theological decline, while a Hungarian's translation of Milne's classic as *Winnie Ille Pu* for precocious children became the only Latin book ever on the *New York Times* best-seller list. In 1897, *Saepius Officio*, the Latin response of the archbishops of Canterbury and York to Leo XIII's *Apostolicae Curae*, which declared Anglican orders invalid, may have been tenuous in argument, but it was widely considered to have been written in a style superior to that of the pontiff. Archbishop Temple was the product of Balliol in Oxford, and Archbishop Maclagan had been at Peterhouse in Cambridge, where Lewis eventually became professor of medieval and Renaissance literature, juggling Latin and Italian.

Lewis was a member of the Inklings circle, along with Dorothy Sayers. She considered her translation of the *Divine Comedy* her best work, while also writing an amusing essay, "The Greatest Single Defect of My Own Latin Education," about her father's introducing her to involutions of classic hexameter at the age of six. She thought eleven was an age too old really to get into it. There is a brilliant section in which she tears apart the reconstructed classical, or "Protestant," pronunciation of Latin that Lewis spoke. There is also an eloquent and insightful book by Fr. Milton Walsh, *Second Friends*, about the acquaintance of Lewis with Msgr. Ronald Knox, who had set a university record for winning the Craven, the Hertford, and the Ireland scholarships in classics, as well as the Gaisford Prize for Greek Verse Composition in 1908 and the Chancellor's Prize for Latin Verse Composition in 1910. While any Latinist compared to Knox would be an epigone, Lewis clearly respected Knox, even though he cultivated Tolkien much more despite the fact that, as Lewis put it, he was reared to be suspicious of papists and philologists and Tolkien was both.

Lewis's correspondence with Calabria went on for about seven years, and after the holy priest died, Lewis wrote at least seven letters to another member of Calabria's religious community, Don Luigi Castelli, who died in 1986 at the age of ninety-six. Learning of Calabria's death, Lewis referred to him in a message to Castelli with what I suspect was a deliberate invocation of the phrase about "the dearly departed" that Horace used to console Virgil on the death of Quinctilius Varus: *tam carum caput.* It appears as well in Sir Walter Scott's *Waverley* novels. Lewis had an unfortunate habit of throwing out letters he received when he thought he might otherwise betray confidences. So what we have are only what he sent. The letters are a radiant model of philia friendship, which he described in his 1958 radio talks:

> In friendship ... we think we have chosen our peers. In reality a few years' difference in the dates of our births, a few more miles between certain houses, the choice of one university instead of another ... the accident of a topic being raised or not raised at a first meeting—any of these chances might have kept us apart. But, for a Christian, there are, strictly speaking, no chances. A secret master of ceremonies has been at work. Christ, who said to the disciples, "Ye have not chosen me, but I have chosen you," can truly say to every group of Christian friends, "Ye have not chosen one another but I have chosen you for one another." The friendship is not a reward for our discriminating and good taste in finding one another out. It is the instrument by which God reveals to each of us the beauties of others.

Lewis, himself an Irishman, measured Europe's slothful indifference to the gospel, and anticipated what is now Ireland's bitter adolescent rebellion against it, in his day when Ireland's present decay was then unthinkable. A year before Calabria died, he received a letter from his Oxford friend dated September 15, 1953: "Ergo plerique homines nostri temporis amiserunt non modo lumen supernaturale, sed etiam lumen illud naturale quod pagani habuerunt." (Therefore many men of our time have lost not only the supernatural light, but also the natural light which the pagans possessed.) Earlier that same year he had written in much the same vein, and it is clear that he was thinking out a theory that became a core of his inaugural address "De Discriptione Temporum" in Cambridge on November 29, 1954: "Nunc enim non erubescunt de adulterio, proditione, perjurio, furto, certisque flagitiis quae non dico Christianos doctores, sed ipsi pagani et barbari reprobaverunt." (For now they do not blush at adultery, treachery, perjury, theft, and other crimes, which I will not say Christian doctors, but the pagans and barbarians have themselves denounced.) The hostile reaction of many to his Cambridge address was only more muted and sophisticated than the angry condemnation of Solzhenitsyn's commencement address in 1978 in the newer Cambridge. In vindication of these men's warnings, it is a fact that such remarks would not be tolerated today even in many universities that indulge a delusional claim still to be Catholic.

In his *Confessions*, St. Augustine is a bit embarrassed about the sensitivity of his boyhood when he wept at Virgil's description of the sorrows of Dido, but the polyphonic character of his writing is directly out of the *Aeneid,* just as the speeches of Lincoln have the cadences of the King James Bible and Shakespeare, of whom he could quote reams. The rhythmic correspondence of the Oxford don and the priest of Verona reminds us, among other things, of the collapse of letter writing as a litmus of culture. For many now, the only mail is email. Text messaging deletes rumination, and blocks any inner Cicero.

Assembling the thoughts above has been a little exercise in nostalgia for this writer. I knew neither of the pen pals, but I can say I knew them sort of collaterally. I did know close friends and students of Lewis, including the kindly bishop, Crispian Hollis, with whom I lived for a while and assisted; his father's biography of Thomas More was translated into Italian by Calabria's friend Don Luigi Pedrollo. Then there was Tolkien's eldest son, John, a priest and a most amiable man with many stories of his own. A mentor to me was Elizabeth Anscombe, whose famous debate with Lewis on miracles has been misrepresented: they esteemed and helped each other a lot. Anscombe recalled:

Our Peculiar Times

The meeting of the Socratic Club at which I read my paper has been described by several of his friends as a horrible and shocking experience which upset him very much. Neither Dr Havard (who had Lewis and me to dinner a few weeks later) nor Professor Jack Bennett remembered any such feelings on Lewis' part.

The Modernist theologian Dennis Nineham of Keble College sparred unsuccessfully with Lewis and once, when he visited me on a trip to the United States, expressed to me great irritation that Lewis had become so popular among the young. His discomfort with Lewis was not rare among the local dons, who enlivened the line that "a prophet is not without honor except in his own town" (see Mark 6:4). If anyone surpassed Lewis in some ways of contemplation, it was the amiable Austin Farrer, to whom Lewis dedicated his *Reflections on the Psalms* and who ministered at his deathbed. There were others, or as Latin letter writers would say in a generally accessible way, "et cetera."

Lewis wrote about miracles. Calabria worked them. One miracle was officially recognized in 1986 and another in 1997. On April 18, 1999, "for the honour of the Blessed Trinity, the exaltation of the Catholic faith and the increase of the Christian life, by the authority of our Lord Jesus Christ, and of the Holy Apostles Peter and Paul, and our own, after due deliberation and frequent prayer for divine assistance, and having sought the counsel of many of our brother Bishops," Pope John Paul II declared and defined Giovanni Calabria a saint.

Having married rather late in life, Lewis mourned his wife of a few years. He got an emotive book out of his grief, which one who was never a widower may be forgiven for thinking a bit overwrought. But Don Luigi was more indulgent and offered patient consolation after Lewis wrote in 1961 that he was journeying in solitude through this valley of tears.

When C. S. Lewis Befriended a Living Catholic Saint

In an essay in *The Weight of Glory*, Lewis comments: "The worldlings are so monotonously alike compared with the almost fantastic variety of the saints." The grave of C. S. Lewis in the Holy Trinity churchyard in Headington, Oxford, is very like the quiet place that moved Gray to write his elegy. It is very unlike the tomb of St. Giovanni Calabria's repose in a Baroque land. There is no formal decree about the last state of the professor's soul, but one may entertain an informal assumption that letters once passed between him and the saint *in hac lacrimarum valle* were not the end of the correspondence.

June 6, 2018

A Faithful Pope of the Enlightenment

In the early 1950s, children watched the puppet show *Kukla, Fran, and Ollie* broadcast from Chicago all the way to the Eastern seaboard through the innovative marvel of television. It was more of a children's show for adults, for how else could the sophisticated puns make sense, or what child could understand how Ollie the Dragon confused "The Mikado" with "Madame Butterfly"? Beulah the Witch was a puppet of a mien too ridiculous to frighten any but the most neurasthenic child. One day she threw down her broomstick and declared that she had decided to abandon witchcraft for the wonderful world of empiricism.

A psychologist, Steven Pinker, author of the new book *Enlightenment Now: The Case for Science, Reason, Humanism and Progress* seems bemusingly ignorant of how the case of religion as a benevolent partner of empirical science has been addressed eloquently and convincingly over the past several generations. His notion of reason and science is that they are the other side of the coin of religion and faith, not symbiotic but hostile, with physics unmasking the pretensions of metaphysics. This flies in the face of the fact that most of the nurturers of new knowledge in the eighteenth century were devout religionists. Has he ever heard of Bacon and Newton and Locke, Montesquieu, Adams, and de Tocqueville? And does that caricature of the "Enlightenment" consider that autonomous human reason became the engine of a Reign of Terror and its sequels in the gulags, eugenics, and cultural revolutions of the twentieth century?

If priests in the so-called Age of Enlightenment were sorcerers like Beulah the Witch before she came to her senses, there is the contradictory figure of Pope Benedict XIV who threw down no broom but raised a crozier in the name of the Divine Logos, "the true light that enlightens every man" (John 1:9). This Prospero Lorenzo Lambertini (1675–1758) was born in Bologna, where his tutors set him on a course that would shape him as one of the greatest scholars in the history of the papacy. The Benedictine pioneer in paleontology and archeology, Bernard de Montfaucon, master of Greek and Hebrew, said of the eident prodigy: "Young as he is, he has two societies: one for science and the other for society." Montfaucon was not a social butterfly, but he quickly summed up Lambertini's elegant admixture of scholar and *saloniste*, for whom there was no tension between the library and the drawing room, and whose amiability made him like one of the Chestertonian angels able to fly because they take themselves lightly.

As bishop of Ancona, he enjoyed the devotion of the clergy, and when he was transferred to his native Bologna, his cheerfulness was a tonic for the ills of discontent among some of the priests. It was said that none left his presence sad or angry, and even the less studious among them felt honored by the time he spent reforming the seminary curriculum, with more emphasis on Sacred Scripture and patrology.

In August of 1740, Lambertini was one of fifty-four cardinals who had struggled and intrigued for six months to elect a pope. The days were baking hot and, though news traveled slowly, that year saw Frederick II assume power in Prussia and the song "Rule Britannia" first sung at Cliveden. Adam Smith began studies at Oxford; George Whitfield brought Methodism to the colony of Georgia; and the University of Pennsylvania was founded, shortly after the

Royal Academy of Sciences in Stockholm. Finally Lambertini rose and said in weary jest: "If you wish to elect a saint, choose Gotti; a statesman, Aldobrandini; an honest man, elect me." The joke turned on him and the 247th pope was astonished and somewhat befuddled, but not shy about accepting.

Some thought he conceded too much to foreign interests, but it was never at the expense of the Church's legitimate rights in promotion of the gospel. It became difficult for the most virulent foes of the papacy to resist the charm of his humor and brilliance, and the local Romans enjoyed passing along his jokes and bons mots. When informed of a rumor that the antichrist had been born into the world and was three years old, he replied: "In that case, I shall let my successor handle the problem." Complex matters of revenues required reform of banking systems and regulation of usurious corruption. Daunting was the corruption in the Papal States, especially since the coffers had been exhausted by his predecessors Benedict XIII and Clement XII. Lambertini restructured the administration of his territories, promoted agricultural reforms, and frequently walked among the poorest people in the most dangerous neighborhoods. With common sense, he was lenient in implementing censures of the neuralgic clients of Jansenism. While monies were raised to fight Muslim pirates off Tripoli, the pope had a graceful correspondence with the "Good Turk." Not hasty in lifting social and financial restrictions against Jews, he at least enjoined the Polish bishops to resist anti-Semitic pogroms, and declared that the "blood libel" against Jews was a lie.

Lambertini invented what we know as encyclicals, and his are models of precise thought and clearly identified purpose, reflecting his Thomistic formation. As an example, *Vix Pervenit* considers the problem of usury in a concise and balanced manner, being careful to correct extreme views on the subject with admirable brevity. Perhaps only Innocent IV came close to him as the greatest canon lawyer to occupy the papacy. *Magnae Nobis Admirationis* set the standard for canonical treatment of marriages between Catholics and Protestants, and his laws for canonization lasted right into the twentieth century. Because of their gravity, he was careful that canonizations not be rushed, but warned:

> If anyone dared to assert that the Pontiff had erred in this or that canonization, we shall say that he is, if not a heretic, at least temerarious, a giver of scandal to the whole Church, an insulter of the saints, a favourer of those heretics who deny the Church's authority in canonizing saints, savouring of heresy by giving unbelievers an occasion to mock the faithful, the assertor of an erroneous opinion and liable to very grave penalties.

He instinctively would have been cautious about canonizing popes in rapid succession *subito* lest the practice become like the "apotheosis" of Roman emperors, which was a hint of decay in the imperial dynasties. That flexibility of the pantheon had made sober Roman citizens cynical, as was Vespasian himself: "Vae, puto deus fio!" (Woe is me, I think I am becoming a god!)

Anyone who imagines that the liturgical books were sealed for all ages, like a fly in amber, by Pope St. Pius V should note that a cataract of changes followed Trent, inciting the liturgical conservatism of Benedict XIV to sulfurous contempt. It was in fact the only one of his many attentions that beclouded his sunny nature. He opposed the changes to the liturgical calendar, multiple collects, and the number of new Breviary offices with the rank of "duplex." The only addition he permitted during all of his eighteen years as pope was to bestow the title of Doctor on Leo the Great. There was a plan to simplify the Breviary, to make it more practical for parochial use, but the resulting four-volume study was so vast that the task was abandoned, save for a reform of the *Roman Martyrology*. The Stations of the Cross that the pope erected in the Colosseum stood until they were destroyed by the Italian government in 1870.

An encyclical of 1749, *Annus Qui Hunc*, gave guidelines to sacred music, denouncing the profane music that had crept into churches; ordered an end to informality and undignified celebrations; and even corrected neglect of proper clerical dress. Much of what exists today in the structures of the Melchites and Maronites are the fruit of Lambertini. Humility did not tax his love for the beauty of the Mass, whose ceremonials he embellished, knowing the evangelical power of splendor, while prudence mastered the art of pomp without pomposity. He saw the dangers of false humility in advertising austerity, just as he had little use for the kind of uninformed aestheticism that caricatures aesthetics.

The enlightened pope championed the classical Christian ideal of women's rights free of the enormities of modern feminism, encouraging women in science and mathematics, beginning at the university in his native Bologna even before becoming pope. He enrolled the female pioneer in Newtonian physics and electricity, Laura Bassi, in his group of twenty-five leading intellectuals, his "Benedettini," charged with promoting theoretical physics and other sciences. And as a proper liturgist as well as feminist, he abhorred any ideological manipulation of the liturgy as deeply as he resented the politicization of physical science. In so many words, he understood the "theology of the body" before that awkward term was invented and appropriated by half-educated lecturers on the subject.

Consequently, Benedict opposed attempts to invert the anthropology of the sacred rites. He decreed in the encyclical *Allatae Sunt* of July 26, 1755:

> Pope Gelasius in his ninth letter (chap. 26) to the bishops of Lucania condemned the evil practice which had been introduced of women serving the priest at the celebration of

Mass. Since this abuse had spread to the Greeks, Innocent IV strictly forbade it in his letter to the bishop of Tusculum: "Women should not dare to serve at the altar; they should be altogether refused this ministry." We too have forbidden this practice in the same words in Our oft-repeated constitution *Etsi Pastoralis*. (no. 29)

Lambertini has as great a claim as any pontiff for having founded the Vatican Museums, as well as establishing four academies for the study of antiquities, canon law, and liturgy, plus augmenting the Vatican Library with, among other works, the Ottoboniani treasury of 3,300 volumes. By one measure, he was a micromanager, but an edifying one, examining candidates in the Roman College for the chairs of mathematics and chemistry that he endowed, while he also supervised the publication of the works of Galileo. In matters academic and spiritual, he cast a suspicious eye on the Jesuits, and entrusted a reform of the order in 1758 to Cardinal Saldanha, but that ceased with his death. He never admitted a Jesuit to the College of Cardinals.

Rationalists and skeptics widely respected his knowledge of the world uncontaminated by an inferior worldliness, fascinated by the right way he told them that they were wrong. He suffered fools gladly without making them feel foolish. Of a balanced temper, he had no capacity for sarcasm or insult, and cajoled rather than humiliated. When the French ambassador Choiseul presumed to instruct him on the appointment of bishops, he took the surprised man by the arm and placed him on the papal chair: "Fa' il Papa." (You be the pope.) Even the intimidating empress Maria Theresa was bedazzled by the elegance of the pope's mind and manners, and King George II permitted the free publication of his letters in England. Hard as it is to believe, Voltaire fell under his spell and composed a distich in his honor:

A Faithful Pope of the Enlightenment

> Lambertinius hic est Romae decus, et pater orbis,
> Qui mundum scriptis docuit, virtutibus ornat.

In a match of wits, Lambertini's erudite reply ended with what must be the only instance of a papal blessing for the atheists' favorite prophet:

> The distich has been published at Rome, and objected to by one of the literati, who, in a public conversation, affirmed that there was a mistake in it with regard to the word hic, which is made short, whereas it ought to be always long. To which I replied, that it may be either long or short; Virgil having made it short in this verse: "Solus hic inflexit sensus, animumque labantem." And long in another, "Hic finis Priami fatorum, hic exitus illum." The answer I think was pretty full and convincing, considering that I have not looked into Virgil these fifty years. The cause, however, is properly yours; to your honor and sincerity, therefore, of which I have the highest opinion, I shall leave it to be defended against your opposers and mine, and here give you my apostolical benediction.

And lest anyone think that this tribute to "Lambertini, the father of the world and adornment of Rome, who teaches that world by his writings and honors it by his virtues" was just calculated flattery, the same Voltaire dedicated to him his play *Mahomet* in 1741: "To the head of the true religion, a writing against the founder of all that is false and barbaric." Lord Chesterfield, whose antennae were attuned to subtleties, suggested that Voltaire was being ironic here. Howbeit, Voltaire had nothing bad to say about the pope, but what he did say about the false Prophet was acidic enough for Muslims to protest in the street in Ain, France, when the play was revived in 2005. Horace Walpole, an inspirer of the

Gothic Revival that stood as a rebuke to the Enlightenment, was compelled by this congenial child of "the true light that enlightens every man" (John 1:9):

> Beloved By Papists
> Esteemed By Protestants
> A Priest Without Insolence or Interestedness
> A Prince Without Favourites
> A Pope Without Nepotism
> An Author Without Vanity
> In Short A Man,
> Whom Neither Wit Nor Power Could Spoil
>
> The Son Of A Favourite Minister
> But One Who Never Courted A Prince,
> Nor Worshipped A Churchman,
> Offers In A Free Protestant Country
> This Deserved Incense
> To The Best Of Roman Pontiffs
> MDCCLVII

A cordial evening with the three most brilliant successors of St. Peter might include the polymath Sylvester II, this Benedict XIV (matched for wit perhaps only by Leo XIII), and the second Benedict after him. Exactly one hundred years before Lambertini died, a beleaguered cavalier, Sir Thomas Browne, published *Hydriotaphia*, a study of ancient funerary urns in Norfolk, England. Its dedication to "the ancient of Dayes, the Antiquaries truest object, unto whom the eldest parcels are young, and earth itself an Infant," could have been written by the pope who was bright enough to know how little he knew, and was grateful for knowing it.

April 26, 2018

The Mathematical Innovations
of Fr. Antonio Spadaro

Nearly fifty years ago, my parish secretary, who was elderly even then, kept the parish accounts using an abacus. I gave her the latest kind of electric adding machine, which she used dutifully, but I noticed that she then checked the results with her abacus, an instrument that has been reliable since long before the invention of Hindu-Arabic written numerals. Until then, ten human fingers provided a decimal system.

If we don't get numbers right, we will not get much else right. This is a point Lewis Carroll made in his *Adventures of Alice in Wonderland*. An apocryphal story claims that Queen Victoria, having enjoyed the Alice tales, requested a first edition of Carroll's next book, and was perplexed when it arrived: *An Elementary Treatise on Determinants*. There is a convincing thesis that Carroll, as an Oxford mathematician, wrote Alice's Wonderland adventures to satirize new non-Euclidean theories. For instance, when Alice expands to nine feet and shrinks to three inches, she tells the Caterpillar, "Being so many different sizes in a single day is very confusing." The Caterpillar enjoys the confusion, which is Carroll's way of saying that Euclidean and hyperbolic geometry, rooted as they are in different axioms, cannot both be true at the same time.

Our Peculiar Times

The guests at the Mad Hatter's tea party are very likely symbolic commentaries on the discovery of quaternions by the Irish mathematician William Rowan Hamilton in 1843.

The abstract algebra, which Carroll thought ridiculous, was the background of Hamilton's theory of "pure time," which he seems to have inferred from Kant's concept of a Platonic ideal of time distinct from chronological time. But this does not deny the existence of time as we know it. Kant himself was almost neurotically compulsive about timing every action of his day by his clock.

One wonders what Carroll would have thought of Einstein's relativity, or Heisenberg's uncertainty principle. But Einstein did not expect that his theory in physics should provide any moral structure, and Heisenberg would not apply a principle of quantum mechanics to theological systems. Since then, many have made such mistakes, the first being the early Modernists and now an increasing number of people even in the heart of Rome, who muddle sciences and hold certainty suspect.

Fr. Antonio Spadaro, a close associate of Pope Francis, raised eyebrows in July 2017 when he described religious life in the United States with such confidence that can come only from a profound knowledge of a subject or a total lack of it. Fr. Spadaro advises the Holy Father, who had never visited the United States before becoming pope. In an essay in *Civiltà Cattolica* called "Evangelical Fundamentalism and Catholic Integralism," Fr. Spadaro spoke with disdain of a cabal formed by Evangelicals and Catholics motivated by a "triumphalist, arrogant, and vindictive ethnicism," which is creating an "apocalyptic geopolitics." Religious fundamentalists behind this plot have included Nixon, Reagan, Bush, and Trump, who is a Manichean. The co-author of this imaginative literary exercise was a Protestant minister, Marcelo Figueroa, who is editor-in-chief of the new Argentinian edition of *L'Osservatore Romano*, to which office he brings the rich systematic theology of

Argentinian Presbyterianism. The two authors were rhetorically florid in denouncing Yankee racism, obscurantism, and fascism, so unlike the temperate history of Spadaro's own peninsula and Figueroa's Argentinian utopia. If they want to condescend to the United States, they need a loftier platform.

Then, in October 2017, Fr. Spadaro said in Boston, "It is no longer possible to judge people on the basis of a norm that stands above all." The suggestion is that a mathematical principle of uncertainty also applies to theology, where all is in flux and subjective.

Later, in a well-publicized comment on Twitter, which operates according to stable and constant principles of applied engineering, Fr. Spadaro typed: "In theology 2 + 2 can equal 5. Because it has to do with God and the real life of people."[11] To put a charitable gloss on that, he may have simply meant theology applied to pastoral situations, where routine answers of manualists may be inadequate. But he has made his arithmetic a guide to dogma, as when he said in his Boston speech that couples living in "irregular" family situations "can be living in God's grace, can love and also grow in a life of grace." Yet, despite his concern for freedom of thought and expression, Fr. Spadaro has recently expressed sympathy for calls to censor Catholic television commentators who insist that 2 + 2 = 4.[12]

There are two things to consider here. First, some clergy of Fr. Spadaro's vintage grew up in a theological atmosphere of "transcendental Thomism." Aquinas begins the *Summa Theologica* asserting in the very first question, four times, that theology has a greater

[11] Quoted in Joel R. Gallagher, "Antonio Spadaro, S.J.: 'Bertrand Russell is the Pope!'," *Crisis Magazine*, April 19, 2017, https://www.crisismagazine.com/2017/antonio-spadaro-s-j-bertrand-russell-pope.

[12] Claire Chretien, "Papal Advisor Retweets Call for Church to Shut Down EWTN Unless They Fire Raymond Arroyo," LifeSite News, February 20, 2018, https://www.lifesitenews.com/news/papal-advisor-retweets-call-for-pope-to-shut-down-ewtn-unless-they-fire-ray.

certitude than any other science. While it gives rise to rhymes and song, it is solid science, indeed the queen of sciences. Transcendental Thomism was Karl Rahner's attempt to wed Thomistic realism with Kantian idealism. Fr. Stanley Jaki, theologian and physicist, called this stillborn hybrid "Aquikantianism." But if stillborn, its ghosts roam corridors of ecclesiastical influence. This really is not theology but theosophy, as romantic as Teilhard de Chardin, as esoteric as a Rosicrucian, and as soporific as the séances of Madame Blavatsky. The second point is that not all cultures have an instinct for pellucid expression. The Italian language is so beguiling that it can create an illusion that its rotundity is profundity, and that its neologisms are significant. When it is used to calling you a "Cattolico integralista" or a "restauratore" the cadences almost sound like a compliment. Even our Holy Father, who often finds relief from his unenviable burdens by using startling expressions, said on June 19, 2016: "We have a very creative vocabulary for insulting others."

In saying that 2 + 2 = 5, Fr. Spadaro preserves a familiar if de-luded intuition, and trailing behind him is a long line of children who in countless schoolrooms have been made to stand in corners for having made that mistake. A famous use of it was in George Orwell's *1984*, speaking of its dystopia: "In the end the Party would announce that two and two made five and you would have to believe it. It was inevitable that they should make that claim sooner or later; the logic of their position demanded it ... the very existence of external reality, was tacitly denied by their philosophy."

Malleable arithmetic has its consequences in the solid world. There is Stalin's consoling wisdom for apparatchiks: "One death is a tragedy; a million is a *statistic*." Unlike Orwell's dystopia, the Third Reich was a fact, and in it, any science that was not ideological was bourgeois. In 1934, the senior German mathematician David Hilbert was asked by the Nazi minister of education, Bernhard Rust, "How is mathematics at Göttingen, now that it is free from the Jewish influence?" Hilbert answered, "There is no mathematics in Göttingen anymore." Imagine mathematics free from Catholic influence. To name but a few devout Catholics who transformed mathematics while confident that 2 + 2 = 4 instead of 5, even in theology, Fr. Spadaro notwithstanding, there are: Fibonacci, Grosseteste, Albertus Magnus, Bacon, Thomas Bradwardine, Oresme, Brunelleschi, Nicholas of Cusa, Regiomantanus, Widmann, Copernicus, Tartaglia, Cardano, Ferrari, Descartes, Pascal, Saccheri, Cauchy, and Bolzano. My favorites are Pope Sylvester II, who revived the decimal numeral system a thousand years ago, and the pioneer woman in mathematics, Maria Agnesi (d. 1799), who refined differential and integral calculus.

The Incarnate Christ subjected Himself to His own laws of nature, including solid arithmetic. He kept count. He insisted that the Twelve not be eleven or thirteen. If 2 + 2 were 5 for Him, He might have said: "When 2½ or 3¾ are gathered together, I am in the midst of them." When He multiplied the loaves, He might have fed 5,000 instead of 4,000, with 8¾ baskets left over, and after 6,250 were fed instead of 5,000, there might have been 15 baskets left over. And we would have a longer workweek, because God rested on the 8.75th day.

The late Vietnamese cardinal Nguyen Van Thuan said that in a certain sense, Jesus actually was a bad mathematician: "A shepherd had 100 sheep; one of them strayed. Without thinking, the shepherd went in search of it, leaving the other 99 sheep. When he found the lost sheep he put it on his shoulders (Luke 15: 4–5). For Jesus, 1 equals 99, perhaps even more." The cardinal could say that without distorting reality because he spent thirteen years in a Communist prison, nine of them in solitary confinement. Those are the real numbers of real years not spent in Wonderland.

February 22, 2018

The Clarity of Cardinal Cupich

Cardinal Blase Cupich of Chicago is all for clarity. It has been a
consistent theme, as when in September of 2017 he issued a decree
banning guns in all parishes, schools, and other facilities across the
archdiocese "so there would be absolute clarity on our position."
His official statement put "clarity" in italics. When he was bishop
of Rapid City, he called for "civility and clarity" in discussing legislation that would limit abortion, but he was somewhat unclear
in explaining that the law "must recognize both the suffering of
the unborn children in abortion and the suffering of the pregnant
women in dire circumstances." The bill was defeated 55 percent
to 45 percent. As bishop of Spokane, he spoke clearly in prohibit-
ing the use of the traditional Latin liturgical books in the Paschal
Triduum. He made very clear his disapproval of seminarians' and
priests' demonstrations against Planned Parenthood: "Decisions
about abortion are not usually made in front of clinics." In 2012, his
pastoral letter on a state referendum to legalize same-sex "marriage"
said: "I also want to be very clear that in stating our position the
Catholic Church has no tolerance for the misuse of this moment to
incite hostility towards homosexual persons or promote an agenda
that is hateful and disrespectful of their human dignity."

Clarity requires effort because it requires honesty, which can
be a costly commodity. So George Orwell said: "The great enemy

of clear language is insincerity. When there is a gap between one's real and one's declared aims, one turns as it were instinctively to long words and exhausted idioms, like a cuttlefish spurting out ink." Clear expression issues from clear thinking, which in turn requires conforming thought to reality. This was a primary concern of the Master in His holy agony, for He prayed to the Father that His Church never fudge the truth: "Sanctify them in the truth; thy word is truth" (John 17:17).

The superior of the Society of Jesus, Fr. Arturo Sosa Abascal, seems wary about the unclear tenor of Christ's teaching about marriage (Matt. 19: 3–9), because "no one had a recorder to take down his words." Consequently, what Christ said must be "contextualized," because human reality "is much more nuanced" and "never black and white." Jesus did say, without the benefit of recorders other than the evangelists: "Heaven and earth will pass away, but my words will not pass away" (Matt. 24:35). There is nothing nuanced about that, but Jesus was not a member of the Society of Jesus.

In an interview the day before he lectured on Pope Francis's exhortation *Amoris Laetitia* at the Von Hügel Institute for Critical Catholic Inquiry in Cambridge, on February 9, Cardinal Cupich hoped that his words "might bring some clarity for people who have raised questions, and then also to raise a challenge for them to also take a second look at the document." In the lecture itself the cardinal quoted *Amoris Laetitia*: "Many people feel that the Church's message on marriage and family does not clearly reflect the preaching and attitudes of Jesus, who set forth a demanding ideal yet never failed to show compassion and closeness to the frailty of individuals" (no. 38). A year earlier, on February 14, 2017, Cardinal Cupich said that the pope's exhortation "expresses with absolute clarity marriage doctrine in full fidelity to traditional Church teaching." One supposes that Cardinal Cupich's lecture in Cambridge was intended to explain why the exhortation's clarity was unclear to so many around the world, even though they have the benefit of recording machines and all the social media, which Jesus lacked, although His voice could be heard by thousands on hilltops and seashores.

In the Von Hügel lecture, which was recorded and thus cannot be nuanced, Cardinal Cupich said by way of apophasis that "it goes without saying" and then went on to say that *Amoris Laetitia* will also mean rejecting "an authoritarian or paternalistic way of dealing with people that lays down the law, that pretends to have all the answers, or easy answers to complex problems, that suggests that general rules will seamlessly bring immediate clarity." There is clarity again, in all its frustrating opaqueness. And after rejecting authoritarianism and paternalism, the cardinal invoked Vatican II's dogmatic constitution on the Church to declare that an innovative interpretation of *Amoris Laetitia* by the bishops of Buenos Aires, by virtue of "the publication in *Acta Apostolicae Sedes* [sic]" of the papal letter commending it, qualifies as an official Church teaching "which all are obliged to abide by and be in conformity with" (*Lumen Gentium*, no. 25).

It should be, and I think it is, clear as night and day that Jesus would not have been crucified had He been more nuanced. There are those who have twisted themselves into pretzels trying to make clear by subtlety, with their own frail command of classical letters, that the official Latinity of *Amoris Laetitia* proves that it is faithful to authentic doctrine, and is not as flawed as its critics claim. This is on a par with Edgar Nye's opinion that Wagner's music is better than it sounds. Such excuses are defeated by Pope Francis himself, who told those Argentinian bishops that their eisegesis "explains precisely the meaning of Chapter VIII."

Cardinal Cupich called *Amoris Laetitia* a "radical change," and Cardinal Parolin said, "It's a paradigm shift and the text itself insists on this, that's what is asked of us—this new spirit, this new

approach!" The exclamation point conveys His Eminence's enthusiasm. Cardinal Cupich asks for a more "holistic" application of the
gospel, in fact using the term ten times without a clear definition
of what it means. There have indeed been paradigm shifters in
Christology, but there have been no Doctors of the Church among
them, and none has been salubrious in the annals of grace. To skim
the surface, they have included Arius, Nestorius, Priscillian, Montanus, Muhammed, Peter Waldo, Luther, Calvin, Jansen, Joseph
Smith, and Phineas Quimby, who coached Mrs. Eddy.

Those who have studied the Early Modernist period might assume that the Von Hügel Institute has as its eponym Baron Friedrich
von Hügel, mentor of the Modernists Alfred Loisy and George
Tyrrell. Actually, it was named for his brother, Anatole, who was
a distinguished naturalist. The baron himself managed to keep his
balance, while using the active if neurasthenic minds of younger
theologians like guinea pigs, watching them degrade while maintaining his own claims to fidelity. The tedious von Hügel (even
his English writings are cadenced as impenetrably German) visited
John Henry Newman at least three times, and on each of these occasions he found Newman melancholy, concluding that Newman
could not be a saint since saints must be joyful. "I used to wonder
how one so good, and one who had made so many sacrifices to God,
could be so depressing." One biographer remarked with astuteness
beyond the reach of the humorless baron, that the only evidence
we have of Newman's being demonstrably depressed was when he
was visited by von Hügel.

This writer writes these words hastily, and knowingly exposes
himself to imputations of illogic, irascibility, and uncharity. Of
only the last I vitally excuse myself, for I mean no irreverence or
ill intent as a parish priest commenting on superiors. In the fullness of charity, I suppose that Cardinal Cupich is so occupied with
the essential works of mercy incumbent upon a spiritual leader of

The Clarity of Cardinal Cupich

many, that he may have availed himself of the advice of others inadequate to the task of preparing his attempts at clarification. The one complaint I invoke, albeit a strong one since much of my life's studies have been nurtured by an intuitive friendship with John Henry Newman, who in an unworthy simile is to me as Philip Neri was to him, is that Cardinal Cupich has cited Newman on conscience to represent the very opposite of what Newman lived and exhausted himself to declare: that conscience must be informed by the Holy Ghost and not left to wander about like a ghost of the subjective human ego, validating uninformed impulses. In his *Letter to the Duke of Norfolk*, Newman distinguished between the operation of conscience and the exercise of private judgment. Such distinctions may be too delicate for hasty doctors of theology, but they are matters for which men were made martyrs. Errors must not be the template for the formation of consciences innocent and malleable. Chesterton warned: "The more doubtful we are about whether we have any truth, the more certain we are (apparently) that we can teach it to children. The smaller our faith in doctrine, the larger is our faith in doctors."

In his revision of the *Arians* book, Newman explained in more detail what he meant by consulting the faithful on doctrine, and it is far different from soliciting the views of confused people who think truths are ideals beyond their reach. As a beacon of clarity, Newman knew that Christ is a Savior and not an Idealist. The word "consult" is, in its Latin root, to consult with or to take counsel in the sense of submission to a truth, as one consults a barometer or takes one's pulse. Newman said this himself. Conscience is not a license for invention or epistemological fabrication, and consultation of the faithful is not a survey to warrant a "paradigm shift." Ronald Knox prefaced his translation of the Bible: "The teaching office of the Holy Spirit does not consist in imparting to the Church the knowledge of hitherto unknown doctrines, in addition to the deposit of faith, but in making our knowledge of doctrines already revealed fuller and more precise."

Cardinal Cupich likes the term "cherry-picking" as a reproach. On February 1 in Holy Name Cathedral, as he had done in 2004 in Rapid City, he faulted pro-lifers for "cherry-picking" instead of accepting the entire "seamless garment" theory. In 2017, he spoke against "cherry-picking" in immigration issues. But *Amoris Laetitia* cherry-picks in citing only one part of the *Summa Theologica* II–II, question 140, in a way that posits the exact opposite of what Aquinas meant,[13] just as Cupich cherry-picks Newman on the "aboriginal vicar of Christ." Cupich cites *Gaudium et Spes*, which calls conscience "the most secret core and sanctuary of a man. There he is alone with God, whose voice echoes in his depths" (no. 16). As Newman was one of the greatest masters of English prose, that kind of lame *poésie* would have appalled him. It also is sourced from a document parts of which Pope Benedict once called downright Pelagian.

The clarification of doctrine is a risky business. In his novel *Loss and Gain*, Newman invented a "little, prim, smirking" character, a preacher in Oxford University named the Rev. Dr. Brownside: "As a divine he seemed never to have had any difficulty in any subject; he was so clear or so shallow that he saw to the bottom of all his thoughts: or, since Dr. Johnson tells us that 'all shallows are clear,' we may perhaps distinguish him by both epithets."

Let us be perfectly clear: Dr. Brownside existed only as a sketch on paper, unlike the Bridegroom of the Church who, even without the corroboration of a recording machine, is believed to have "taught as one having authority and not as the scribes."

February 14, 2018

---

[13] Richard A. Spinello, "The Morality of *Amoris Laetitia* Is Not Thomistic," *Crisis Magazine*, November 14, 2017, https://www.crisismagazine.com/2017/morality-amoris-laetitia-not-thomistic.

The Great Emergency

That every five hundred years the Church passes through a crisis is not a novel insight. It may be something of a contrived schematic, since there have been other crises as well, but each of those periods of crisis has influenced the Church to an extraordinary and radical degree: the fall of the Roman Empire, the great East-West Schism, and the Protestant revolt.

These days there seems to be a "perfect storm" of events that add up to a fourth crisis, and the faithful must trust that "through toil and tribulation" the purging of corrupt elements will result in a stronger Catholic witness. Recently, Pope Francis told the press: "I will not say a word," referring to some of the most serious allegations of decadence in the Church, and he has long declined to respond to the *dubia* of four cardinals on the spiritual economy of marriage. Some have thought that such reticence is inconsistent with his dogmatic outspokenness on ambiguous matters such as climate change and capital punishment. Last New Year's Day, he said: "I would once again like to raise my voice" about immigration, and on Palm Sunday he told young people: "You have it in you to shout" even if "older people and leaders, very often corrupt, keep quiet." This is why there was an eagerness to hear him when in the course of these most tumultuous months, on the fourth World Day of Prayer for the Care of Creation, he finally spoke — but it turned out to be a warning about plastic debris in the world's waters.

On September 1, 2018, this successor of Gregory I, who saw Latin civilization crumbling, and Leo IX, who grieved the loss of Constantinople, and Pius V, who pitied souls lost in the heretical northern lands, implored and lamented: "We cannot allow our seas and oceans to be littered by endless fields of floating plastic. Here, too, our active commitment is needed to confront this emergency." The struggle against plastic litter must be fought "as if everything depended on us."

It was a sobering moment for all who care for what the Holy Father called "the great waters and all they contain." The poignancy of such pastoral solicitude inevitably brings to mind the historic document of the Pontifical Council for the Pastoral Care of Migrants and Itinerant People in 2007, which was entitled: "Guidelines for the Pastoral Care of the Road." It marked precisely the one thousandth anniversary of the no less important peace treaty with the Vikings signed by King Æthelred the Unready. The world will long remember this pontifical document's opening line: "Moving from place to place, and transporting goods using different means, have characterized human behavior since the beginning of history." The guidelines also pointed out that "a vehicle is a means of transport" (no. 21) and observed, "Sometimes the prohibitions imposed by road signs may be perceived as restrictions on freedom" (no. 23). Drawing on generations of pastoral wisdom, the instruction warned: "The fact that a driver's personality is different from that of a pedestrian's should be taken into account" (no. 24) and cautioned against "rude gestures" (no. 27). From their own cultural experiences as Italians, the president of the council, Cardinal Renato Martino, and the council's secretary, Agostino Marchetto, titular archbishop of Astigi, noted that "cars tend to bring out the 'primitive side' of human beings, thereby producing rather unpleasant results" (no. 29).

More than a decade later, there is yet to be realized the council's dream of "periodic celebrations of liturgies at major road points" (no. 82). One hopes that the World Day of Prayer for the Care of Creation will produce more tangible results. There are cynics who would try to dismiss the plastic-pollution emergency as though it were not a "massive, massive crisis." However, the issue will not go away. You might say that the problem has been with us since plastic first appeared in 1284, as a naturally made compound of tortoise shell and horn. And, of course, 1284 was the year that the Lüneburg manuscript first recorded the tale of the Pied Piper of Hamelin, whom the former cardinal Theodore McCarrick, in a lecture at Villanova University in 2013, used as a metaphor for the charism of Pope Francis. He was unaware that 130 children were never seen again after the Piper led them into a cave.

The first man-made plastic, derived from cellulose, was exhibited at the 1862 International Exhibition in London, being the invention of Alexander Parkes. As a specimen of accidental synchronicity, it happened that during the installation of that marvel, the British minister to Rome, Lord Odo Russell, assured an anxious Pope Pius IX that Queen Victoria would grant him asylum in England should he have to flee the Eternal City.

In the 1967 film *The Graduate*, Mr. McGuire tells Benjamin: "Plastics. There's a great future in plastics. Think about it. Will you think about it?" That optimism, born of naïveté about fallen man's abuse of the oceans, is mocked by today's emergency. Condemning the privatization of water resources, Pope Francis implied that a large burden of fault is to be attributed to Western capitalists. However, an awkward fact looms: a 2017 Ocean Conservancy report indicates that more plastic is dumped into the oceans by China, along with Thailand, Indonesia, the Philippines, and Vietnam, than by the entire rest of the world. Indeed, 90 percent of all plastic in the seas and oceans is carried there by rivers in India, Africa, and mostly China. Nonetheless, the chancellor of the Pontifical Academy of Social Sciences, Bishop Marcelo Sanchez Sorondo, has said: "Right now, those who are best implementing the social doctrine of the Church are the Chinese." In China "the economy does not dominate politics, as in the United States," where President Trump is "manipulated" by global industrialists. Shortly before the Chinese government bulldozed yet another church and banned crucifixes, Sorondo declared that China was implementing Pope Francis's encyclical letter *Laudato Si'* better than many countries and "is assuming a moral leadership that others have abandoned."

Plastic is not mentioned in Sacred Scripture, not even in the New American Bible. But we may safely assume that Jesus would have had difficulty walking on water if it had been filled with plastic trash. St. Peter found a gold coin in the mouth of a fish, but today he might very well find only a piece of Styrofoam. When Our Lord fed the five thousand and the four thousand, the leftovers filled twelve and seven *kphinoi*, or wicker baskets, respectively. These were huge crowds, especially if you add the number of women and children, and more so if $2 + 2 = 5$, as Fr. Spadaro has suggested is the case in theology. But the point is: these baskets were biodegradable, and it would never have occurred to the Master to use plastic trash bags, even if such had existed. Eventually the baskets would have decayed and returned to the soil from whence they came. And that is how it should be. Even the parables can be updated for the present emergency: the Good Ecologist, having recycled ninety-nine plastic bottles, still goes out in search of the one polyurethane bottle that is lost.

On the other hand, Our Lord does seem to have had a different concept of moral emergencies, to wit:

Hear me, all of you, and understand: there is nothing outside a man which by going into him can defile him; but the things which come out of a man are what defile him.... For from within, out of the heart of man, come evil thoughts, fornication, theft, murder, adultery, coveting, wickedness, deceit, licentiousness, envy, slander, pride, foolishness. All these evil things come from within, and they defile a man. (Mark 7:14–15, 21–23)

But for many facing the emergency of plastic refuse, that may be a matter for another day.

September 19, 2018

Where Are the Churchmen with Chests?

To have been the proverbial fly on the wall during a conversation, one good time would have been during dinner in the White House on September 2, 1943, when Franklin Roosevelt was hosting Winston and Clementine Churchill with their daughter Mary and the newly appointed ambassador to the Soviet Union, Averell Harriman. The other dinner guest was the future cardinal Archbishop Francis Spellman, just back from a lengthy tour of overseas military units.

Mary was devoted to her father and accompanied him on many wartime trips, including to Quebec, Washington, and Potsdam. In 1966 when I was a student, she befriended me and invited me to Chartwell when it was being prepared for a public opening, and I had time alone with her father's paintings. She was better than any fly on the wall and seemed to have total recall of table talk great and small. The conversation on September 2, fresh from the Quebec Conference, was about the future of Russia. On the next morning, the cardinal had a longer conversation with the president, first about declaring Rome an "open city," a subject the president had addressed in a press conference on July 23, and then about post-war prospects for Eastern Europe, especially Poland. Roosevelt had expressed a desire that Rome be an open city, but cited Nazi Germany and Fascist Italy's opposition to the idea. Spellman would recount the conversation himself. In short, he was taken aback by what Roosevelt said so cavalierly about Soviet designs: "There is no point to oppose these desires of Stalin, because he has the power to get them anyhow. So better give them gracefully." For the cardinal's benefit, Roosevelt hoped "although it might be wishful thinking" that the Russian intervention in Europe "might not be too harsh." Likewise, despite Winston's embrace of Roosevelt, the Soviet threat strained him greatly, and his plangent message when the president died did not obscure his conspicuous absence at the funeral.

Churchill was not to be ranked among the mystics or ascetics of Christendom. He avowed: "I am not a pillar of the church. I am more of a flying buttress: I support it from the outside." His instincts were impatient with the Fathers, but he could be moved to tears by good hymns and carefully prescribed the ones he wanted when he died. Loyalty to the Established Church was a patriotic impulse rather than a matter of faith, for the restless dogmas that supported the Establishment varied with the tides; yet he saw through religious sham enough to avow that if he had become a clergyman, he would have enjoyed unsettling the bishops by preaching sermons highly orthodox in character. Of practical ecclesiastical matters he was amusingly ignorant, and in 1942, perhaps only half in jest, he wanted to have Cardinal Hinsley appointed archbishop of Canterbury. But that expression was not insignificant, because he saw in Hinsley's strong voice during the dark war years a manly and indeed prophetic courage that resonated in ways that could save nations as well as souls.

Of interest here is the deference that someone like Spellman or Hinsley could engender from secular leaders not innocent of cynicism but respectful of integrity. It recalls the tribute that the magnificent curmudgeon H.L. Mencken surprisingly paid to Cardinal Gibbons: "A man of the highest sagacity, a politician in the best sense" who never "led the Church into a bog or up a blind alley."

Where Are the Churchmen with Chests?

That kind of virile exemplar would find it hard to take root in the ecclesiastical soil today, notwithstanding some venerable figures. The clerical vacuity that proposes itself as a substitute for apostolic prophecy is especially disappointing, and even dangerous, in our difficult times. In the First World War, Cardinal Mercier said that the sentimental and vapid preaching of his clergy in his tortured country "told the people to love but not why they should do it." There should be unflagging caution when clerics are hauled in to add a pious gloss to a political event, which is why strained and cobbled events such as presidential prayer breakfasts court humbug, but these can also be opportunities for flexing the sinews of the gospel. Nonetheless, on some national civic occasions benign Catholic prelates miss the opportunity and disappoint the faithful by deliberately neglecting the counsel of Luke 12:8–9.

Franklin Roosevelt's fifth cousin once removed did not like Churchill, whom he had met only once and briefly, during the latter's lecture tour as a youth in 1900. Churchill's first offense was that he did not rise when a lady entered the room. Theodore told a friend, "He is not an attractive fellow." Winston was eighteen years younger than Theodore, who had charged up San Juan Hill two months before Churchill had charged at Omdurman, but in ways they were too much alike to get on well. When Churchill published a biography of his father six years later, Teddy's assessment written to Senator Henry Cabot Lodge might have been a sketch of himself: "Still, I feel that, while the biographer and his subject possess some real farsightedness ... both possess or possessed such levity, lack of sobriety, lack of permanent principle, and an inordinate thirst for that cheap form of admiration which is given to notoriety, as to make them poor public servants." Similar words are spoken sniffingly today by the media, superior clerics, and preening intellectuals about a president they think is "heinously unsuitable" and a "connoisseur of low culture" and generally not up to snuff.

Our Peculiar Times

But carrying the heavy baggage of his many calamitous missteps, such as Gallipoli in 1915, Dieppe in 1943, the Bengal famine of 1943, and his ambiguity about the Normandy invasion, Winston could honestly fit the same Roosevelt's 1910 description in a lecture at the Sorbonne:

> The credit belongs to the man who is actually in the arena, whose face is marred by dust and sweat and blood; who strives valiantly; who errs, who comes short again and again, because there is no effort without error and shortcoming; but who does actually strive to do the deeds; who knows great enthusiasms, the great devotions; who spends himself in a worthy cause; who at the best knows in the end the triumph of high achievement, and who at the worst, if he fails, at least fails while daring greatly, so that his place shall never be with those cold and timid souls who neither know victory nor defeat.

These observations provoke an anxious solicitude for the present state of the Church, for it would be hard to find a surplus of Church leaders in the arena of such men. The common instinct for Rotarian jocularity rather than true Christian prophecy resembles the manner of Churchill's home secretary, Herbert Morrison, whom the prime minster called "A curious mixture of geniality and venom." Those anointed to proclaim Christ seem not infrequently reticent about enlisting His Holy Name in what is no less than spiritual warfare that cannot be won by appeasement. When our bishops were assured by President Obama that there would be no imposition of civil regulations on the Church's moral standards, specifically in matters of health care, they left a meeting in the White House boasting that they had been promised a good deal. It was their Munich. That conjures the ghost of Neville Chamberlain waving his piece of paper securing "peace for our time." When

Chamberlain died, Churchill refused to humiliate his memory and paid an eloquent tribute in the House to his predecessor's virtue, but he could not hide the naïveté that paved the steps winding the way down to near destruction.

As it is a nervous business for prelates to court and be courted by civil power, one might question the wisdom of popes' addressing the United Nations or parliaments. A pope is not merely another head of state, and the whole history of the economy of Christ and Caesar makes clear that popes are never stronger than when they are weakest in things temporal. Surely a man resolved as Pope Francis is to do what is right for mankind was ill-served by those who counseled him on what to say in addressing a joint session of Congress. On that awkward day, the Holy Father spoke of refugees, human rights, the death penalty, natural resources, disarmament, and distribution of wealth, but there was no mention of Jesus Christ. The speech invoked acceptable figures such as Abraham Lincoln, Martin Luther King, Dorothy Day, and Thomas Merton, but no canonized saint that the nation's legacy boasts.

The resources of the Church in the material order are vast, if fading, but her supernatural resources are beyond calculation. An indicting finger points to the neglect of such treasures of talent and grace in lands of privilege, as for example in the mercenary hypertrophy of the Church in Germany. This affects all limbs of the Body of Christ. Where there are bishops of moral vigor, there will be an abundance of young men willing to take up the call of priestly service. Where the spirit is tepid and refreshes itself on the thin broth of a domesticated and politically correct gospel, seminaries will be vacant. As C. S. Lewis gave account: "We make men without chests and expect from them virtue and enterprise. We laugh at honor and are shocked to find traitors in our midst."

In his *Idea of a University*, Newman wrote: "Neither Livy, nor Tacitus, nor Terence, nor Seneca, nor Pliny, nor Quintillian, is an adequate spokesman for the Imperial City. They write Latin; Cicero writes Roman." The Church needs a Roman vigor that persuades men to rise above self-consciousness. An English bishop reflected: "Wherever St. Paul went, there was a riot. Wherever I go, they serve tea." In spiritual combat, there is no teatime, and effective strategies cannot be plotted at conferences, synods, workshops, and costly conventions at resort hotels with multiple "break-out" sessions and mellow music. One fears that a fly on the wall at any of those conversations would drop to the floor out of boredom. "For if the trumpet give an uncertain sound, who shall prepare himself to the battle?" (1 Cor. 14:8, KJV).

January 22, 2018

On the Blithe Ignorance
about the National Anthem

The current neo-Puritanical mania for tearing down statues and stifling free speech by cultural ingénues ignorant of history and logic has reached a stellar absurdity in demands to censure "The Star Spangled Banner" on lame claims that it is racist and advertises bigotry. Given the low level of contemporary culture, it is easy to indulge the fallacy known as "argumentum ad verecundiam" whereby some people, because of celebrity or prowess in a particular field, are taken seriously when they discourse on matters outside their competence. Sports figures who are paid millions of dollars think that their sudden wealth and athletic agility justify their sanctimonious opinions on complex historical matters. If ignorance is bliss, these fellows already have reached nirvana.

It has been alleged by those for whom shabby facts deface pristine theory that our national anthem was the work of a bigot and canonized as our official anthem at the instigation of modern racists. To revise the revisionists, it helps to take a little walk into reality. In 1814, Francis Scott Key penned the words later set to the English song "To Anacreon in Heaven"—a tune that is a challenge to singers, as even Renée Fleming confessed after performing it at the 2014 Super Bowl. It is often mutilated by rock stars calling attention to themselves by "interpreting" it. Personally, since I am not a canary, I prefer other tunes.

"La Marseillaise" is incomparable for stirring even the most lethargic citizen, although its image of flooding fields with impure blood was not meant as a limp metaphor. "God Save the Queen" is so sturdy that Americans have wantonly purloined the melody, and its lines about scattering the queen's enemies, confounding their politics and frustrating their knavish tricks, are not for the faint of heart in the European Union. But they seem to have been a potent tonic for a nonagenarian monarch. By comparison, bombs bursting in air are pretty mild. Key wrote the words after watching 19 British ships fire more than 1,500 cannonballs, mortar shells, and rockets on Baltimore. Key was indeed a slave-owner, but he had a conscience as well as a brain, and when it was quickened he ordered the manumission of his slaves. In 1820 he embarked on the seven-year effort of pleading before the Supreme Court for the liberation of three hundred African slaves captured off the ship *Antelope* along the Florida coast. He also worked with John Quincy Adams in the Amistad case to free fifty-three slaves.

Key's poem "The Defence of Fort McHenry"—which, renamed "The Star-Spangled Banner," became the national anthem in 1931—was based on verses he composed in 1805 to celebrate the victory over the Muslim slave-trading pirates on the Barbary Coast ("the shores of Tripoli"). "And pale beam'd the Crescent, its splendor obscured / By the light of the Star-Spangled flag of our nation.... / And the turban'd heads bow'd to its terrible glare." John Langdon was a Founding Father who, as the first president pro tempore of the Senate, administered the vice-presidential oath of office to John Adams and, as governor of New Hampshire, set aside a day of thanksgiving in 1805 "for the termination of our contest with one of the African powers; the liberation of our fellow-citizens from bondage." One neglected but controverted stanza of the anthem is probably mistaken as a reference to typical slavery, when it most likely addressed The British navy's impressment of seamen. Here, "slave" has nothing to do with race, but means simply "oppression," as in "Rule Britannia," which declared that "Britons never shall be slaves." Those words of John Thomson, by the way, were set to their great melody by the Catholic composer and hymnographer Thomas Arne.

Islam, which means "submission," has never had abolitionists like the Christians Bartolomé de las Casas, Benedict XIV, William Wilberforce, and Daniel O'Connell. Muhammed was a slave-owner and slave-trader, and the Qur'an devotes five times as much space to regulating labor slavery and sex slavery as it does to prayer. Recent revisionist attempts to portray Muhammed as a liberator of slaves falls apart in face of the fact that he is recorded as doing this only in an exchange of two black slaves for one Arab. He often enslaved freemen captured in battle and did not spare women and children. The Qur'an (4:24; 33:52) records a divine mandate from Allah permitting believers an unlimited number of sex slaves. Muhammed himself gave women to his three eventual successors: the caliphs Umar, Uthman, and Ali. As Muhammed is considered the perfect man, none of his actions were faulty, and slavery itself, therefore, even when modified or abolished by civil code, can never be intrinsically wrong, or subject to doctrinal development as offensive to natural law, which does not exist in Islam.

Over fourteen centuries, roughly two hundred million slaves, white and black, were sold by Muslim traders, and almost all the Africans sold to European traders for export to America were enslaved by Muslims. Muslim slavers sought markets during their European invasions, and even raided west county Cork in Ireland, capturing 107 Irish and English villagers from a place called, coincidentally, Baltimore on June 20, 1631, and consigning them to perpetual slavery in North Africa. So many Eastern Europeans were enslaved that the word "slave" itself comes from "Slav." While lip service is given to abolition in Islamic lands, slavery today in the forms of bondage, forced labor, human trafficking, and servile marriage is blatant in Sudan, Niger, The Gambia, Benin, the Ivory Coast, and Senegal. A quarter of the 3.8 million inhabitants of Mauritania, a Sunni state, are slaves. Slavery was not abolished (at least nominally) in Saudi Arabia and Yemen until 1962 under Western pressure, principally from Britain. Actual slavery is common in Hinduism as well, and India has the most slaves among nations: some eighteen million, more than the population of the Netherlands.

Where is the indignation of protestors here? Indignation is selective. The media featured one young Muslim woman, an American citizen, who joined the protest against the national anthem because of its "bigotry." This recalled the objection to the Australian national anthem registered in 2015 by an "Islamic spokesman," Mr. Uthman Badar: "Requiring schoolchildren to sing the national anthem, and the citizenship pledge supporting democratic values, are a part of an oppressive campaign by Australian authorities of 'forced assimilation' of the Muslim community."

Revisionists who burlesque the past and mute the voice of reason fail to recognize that the value of life is secured best by the standard of the Cross and not the Crescent.

September 27, 2017

Pentecost Was Not an Occasion
for "Enthusiasm"

The amiable classicist John Bird Sumner was the Protestant arch-bishop of Canterbury from 1848 to 1862. Amid theological contro-versies about baptismal regeneration and the like, his opposition to a parliamentary bill removing Jewish disabilities was unquestionably retrograde, but he assumed the progressive mantle in approving obstetric anesthesia, which was opposed by some Christian fun-damentalists, whose misogyny was not alien to current Muslim advocates of female circumcision. It will be allowed that he had little choice after Queen Victoria had been anesthetized for the birth of Prince Leopold. As a son of Cambridge rather than Oxford, his propensities were more Evangelical. Nonetheless, he is said to have blessed missionaries to India in the imperial radiance of the Raj with the counsel that they were to "convert the heathen and discourage Enthusiasm."

Now, among the Anglo-Saxon race, one of the more sober insults was to label a man as "hearty." But Enthusiasm understood with a capital "E" was Methodism and its ancillary nonconformist forms, which emphasized emotion over reason.

When the apostles and the women with them in the Upper Room received the Holy Spirit, as promised by the Lord who never lies, they were filled with a power that has changed the world. It did not change their intellect. There is no literature in the classical corpus more replete with incontestable reason obedient to the divine logic than the preaching of the apostles.

Our Lord promised that the Holy Spirit would lead to all truth. This activates the intellect and does not replace it. Enthusiasm is not spiritual zeal if it asks reason to move over so that emotion might take its place. The Enthusiasm that Dr. Sumner abjured displaced the Logos with the Ego. That of course is an old story, elegantly and eloquently documented in the masterwork of Msgr. Ronald Knox, *Enthusiasm*. While not unsympathetic toward the noble integrity of John Wesley, he holds up the spiritist movements from the second-century Montanists to the latter-day Quakers, Jansenists, and Quietists as examples of how people go to extremes to confuse themselves emotionally with the Holy Spirit.

At Pentecost, the apostles spoke the languages of the far-flung regions of the Jewish diaspora. Modern "speaking in tongues" is not the equivalent of the manifestation of real languages. Even when there was such, St. Paul diminished it, subordinating it to interpretation. St. Irenaeus mentions contemporaries who spoke "through the Spirit" in all kinds (*pantodapais*) of tongues. St. Francis Xavier much later preached in tongues he had not learned, but they were real languages and, if one is willing to accept it, on only two occasions: in Travancore and again at Amanguci.

It is curious that the Charismatic movements after the Second Vatican Council should have neglected the Latin of the Universal Church, before affecting exotic and unintelligible speech. As an inveterate and unapologetic New Yorker whose pastoral obligations require speaking various languages, I suggest that a really miraculous gift of the Holy Spirit would enable people in Manhattan to speak grammatical English, the equivalent of the dialect of the diaspora spoken at Pentecost, and the contradiction of faux glossolalia.

Pentecost Was Not an Occasion for "Enthusiasm"

False Pentecostal enthusiasm tries to energize the emotions but not the intellect. It is a wise policy, issuing from experience, and one hopes not from cynicism, to distrust email messages that begin by saying that the writer is "excited to share" something. This inevitably includes an overuse of exclamation points. Mark Twain and F. Scott Fitzgerald equally disdained the use of exclamation points as a kind of laughter at your own jokes. Exclamation points signal a failure to get a sober point across, and are the grammatical equivalent of the vaudeville performers who waved the American flag and held a baby to prevent the bored audience from throwing objects at them.

In religion, various movements that, in practice, move nowhere keep pumping themselves up with excited promises of something great about to happen, some new committee or rally or bureaucratic program for evangelization that blurs the distinction between the good news and novelty.

Such was the case in Phrygia of Asia Minor in what is now Turkey during the second century. A convert priest named Montanus stirred up a lot of excitement when he confused himself with the Holy Spirit and proclaimed various "prophecies" while in a trance, like a sort of divine ventriloquist. In the manner of a typical fanatic so defined, he was confident that God would agree with him if only God had all the facts. In a languid and dissolute period, the local Churches already having become formalistic and arid (contrary to romantic depictions of the uniform zeal of all early Christians, and not unlike the motivation of John Wesley to stir up the dormant Church of England), the ardor of Montanus attracted many as far as North Africa and Rome itself, not all of whom were innocent of neurosis. Even the formidable mind of Tertullian welcomed it. Sensational outbursts of emotion were thought to be divinely inspired, and the formal clerical structure of the Church was caricatured as the sort of rigidity that quenches the Spirit. Avowing that prophecy did not end with the last apostles,

Monatists pronounced new messages and encouraged false speaking in tongues pretending to be actual languages. Women such as Priscilla and Maximilla left their husbands and decided that they could be priestesses and prophetesses.

In the twentieth century, the Montanist heresy sprung up again. The Pentecostal sects and even many Catholics were attracted to "reawakenings" that gave the impression that the Paraclete promised by Christ, who never lied had finally come awake, having slumbered pretty much since the early days of the Church. While its extreme forms were bizarre, such as dancing in churches and uncontrolled laughter and barking like dogs while rolling on the floor, any quest for novelty quickly grows bored, for nothing goes out of fashion so fast as the latest fashion.

In preparing for the celebration of Pentecost, the Church prays for a holy reception of the truth "ever ancient, ever new," which comes not through a second or third Pentecost, but through an embrace of God's timeless grace. Christ makes "all things new" and does not superficially make all new things (see Rev. 21:5).

Heresies are fads. The estimable Servant of God Fr. John Hardon, whose talks would never be called ecstatic, bluntly said that the modern Charismatics are Montanists. It is true that the Charismatic movement in the Catholic Church wisely was blessed insofar as it did not denigrate from or add to authentic dogma. But in the second century, Pope Eleutherius was inclined to condone Montanism, too, until the anti-Tertullian theologian Praxeas explained its problems.

Chesterton described the romance of orthodoxy whose Church is like a chariot "thundering through the ages, the dull heresies sprawling and prostrate, the wild truth reeling but erect." The truth needs no artificial excitement or orchestrated exclamation points, for when the mystery of God is revealed, all and every element in the cataract of creation collapses into silent awe (Rev. 8:1) and then … the Great Amen.

Pentecost Was Not an Occasion for "Enthusiasm"

Christ promised that the Holy Spirit would enable human intelligence to embrace depths of reality beyond the limits of natural experience. Here at work is the principle of St. Thomas Aquinas: "Grace does not destroy nature, but perfects it." The apostles became more intensely human when they received the power of the Holy Spirit, to the extent that they traveled to lands beyond the limited environs of their early years, with a courage never before tested. They received the "glory" that Christ, on the night before He died, prayed that His disciples might share. Because that participation in the divine nature bridges time and eternity, there is an invigorating terror about it: not the dread of being diminished or annihilated, but the trembling awesomeness of breaking the bonds of death itself.

When the Holy Spirit moves a man from aimless biological existence to what Christ calls the "fullness" of life, the reaction is a little like that of someone who has heard simple tunes but then encounters a symphony. Simple pleasures may evoke smiles, but the deepest joys can move one to tears, and that is why there is that curious experience of not laughing but weeping for joy, and the equally enigmatic experience of lovesickness. Oft quoted is the diary account by Samuel Pepys in the seventeenth century after attending a concert: "That which did please me beyond anything in the whole world was the wind-musique when the Angel comes down, which is so sweet that it ravished me; and indeed, in a word, did wrap up my soul so that it made me really sick, just as I have formerly been when in love with my wife."

An admirer of Jascha Heifetz told him after a performance that his violin had such a beautiful tone. The maestro placed his ear against the Stradivarius and said, "I hear nothing." By way of metaphor, it may be said that we exist biologically as wonderful instruments: the brain itself is the most complex organ in the universe. But we make celestial music, attaining the "tone" of virtue, only when the Holy Spirit conjoins our human nature with the Source of Life.

At Pentecost, all who worship God are transfigured by His holy light. No man-made enthusiasm can equal the transporting eloquence of the unutterable Logos. So spoke St. Cyril of Jerusalem: "As light strikes the eyes of a man who comes out of darkness into the sunshine and enables him to see clearly things he could not discern before, so light floods the soul of the man counted worthy of receiving the Holy Spirit and enables him to see things beyond the range of human vision, things hitherto undreamed of."

June 1, 2017

While Only God Is Good,
Everyone Can Be Perfect

The sonorous start of Lent jolts with the reminder that man is dust and shall return to dust. It is hardly what we call news: Abel learned it when Cain struck him, before there were calendars or clocks or Donne's tolling bell. Even the immortals of our civic pantheon and postage stamps were immortalized by way of their shocking mortality.

The daunting fact that God came into the world as a frail baby and left this world as the Risen Lord stretches the short attention span of the human intellect, but there is an instinct to line up for ashes on Wednesday before Lent, because dust is cogent and so, too, is a sense that there is more to life than dust. As a priest for a long while in New York City, invoking my poor arithmetic but adequate memory, I estimate that I have stood in front of altars as at least a quarter of a million people have come to be marked with ash, some of them saints and others spiritual hitchhikers, but all asking, by mutely lining up, "Can these bones live?" (Ezek. 37:3). The answer comes when a breath not of this created world breathes into creatures, and the bones come alive again, "an exceedingly great host" (Ezek. 37:10).

That great host is a metaphor signaling how the Holy Spirit can stir up long-dormant abilities and skills that animate the intellect and will. How, for instance, does one explain the effulgence of cultural innovation after moribund centuries? What explains the Italian Renaissance and the Scottish Enlightenment? It is unlikely that novel powers were at work, or talents sprang anew as from the brow of Zeus. More probably, the breath of God gave life to what was waiting to come alive. What was then can be now. There may be a few Raphaels and Titians nascent in the Bronx, but dormant because untutored; and there may be a Raeburn or a Scott in Chevy Chase or Grosse Pointe, ready to paint and write but distracted by an overbearing mother driving him to soccer practice. On a deeper level, everyone is a potential saint, and that potency can flourish if one does not "quench the Spirit" (1 Thess. 5:19).

One of the longest discussed, and often most harshly argued, questions for Christians has been how much divine breath, that is, saving grace, is needed to give new and unending life to the broken human condition. Possibly from acquaintance with the sort of people one instinctively avoids, the notion that man is "totally depraved" took wide hold in the sixteenth century. But it had already been engaged in the fourth century when, at the very same time there spread the opposite contention that we are better off than we think, and can manage quite well with just a little help from God. That excited the rebukes of men so unlike each other as St. Augustine and the more irascible St. Jerome, who called the mistaken optimist Pelagius "an Irishman overstuffed with porridge." The Irish say he was Welsh, and the Welsh say he was English.

Later, through misreadings of Augustine, not helped by some of that saint's own expressions, self-styled reformers such as Luther and Calvin, and then Bishop Jansen of Ypres in the Catholic sphere, took the more pessimistic view of man's ability to grow in grace. They lost their grip on the original benign form of creation. Like all misguided reformers, as Chesterton said, they knew what was wrong but did not know what was right. All heresies are an exaggeration of a truth, to the exclusion of its subtleties. The Council of Trent affirmed the truth that man cannot be in harmony with God's plan, or "justified," by his own good behavior without the grace of God that comes through Jesus Christ. This is why Christ said that no one is good except God (Mark 10:1). But Trent also rejected the lie that "since Adam's sin, the free will of man is lost and extinguished."

Dry bones and limp lives can come alive by giving God permission (as St. Teresa of Calcutta often said) to make us what He wants us to be. While no one is good except God, anyone can become perfect (Matt. 5:48). This is not a contradiction. Goodness is a quality of being; perfection is the result of contact with that goodness. True goodness is divine; perfection comes by way of being "partakers of the divine nature" (2 Pet. 1:4). A perfect man is not a perfectionist. Perfectionism is a neurosis based on the confusion of goodness and perfection. The perfectionist tries to defy mortality without the help of God who alone is immortal. In the social order, a secular progressive dreams of perfecting an ideal society on earth through human effort, and learns the hard way that utopias end up being hells. After all, for all his cheerfulness, St. Thomas More invented that word because "utopia" means "no place." That is the opposite of the Kingdom of God, which is heavenly without being inaccessible, and earthly without being temporal. To say that God's "center is everywhere and his circumference is nowhere" could fit the vagaries of all sorts of thinkers from Empedocles to Voltaire, but when meant as Nicholas of Cusa used it, God is both transcendent and immanent, and so His immortal goodness can bring to perfection what is mortal.

Antoine de Saint-Exupéry said that perfection is achieved not when there is nothing more to add, but when there is nothing more to take away. (Il semble que la perfection soit atteinte non quand il n'y a plus rien à ajouter, mais quand il n'y a plus rien à retrancher.) Perfectionism tries to add, as though goodness were a sum, while perfection subtracts that which obscured goodness. It is said that Michelangelo explained to a child that he sculpted Moses simply by chipping away from the marble all that was not Moses—but Moses had been there all along.

Exactly two years ago, twenty young Coptic-Christian Egyptians were kidnapped by Islamic State militants while on a work crew in Libya. Lined up on a beach east of Tripoli, and taunted by their captors, they refused to renounce Christ. Defiantly and joyfully, they chanted in chorus, "Ya Rabbi Yasou!" (Oh my Lord Jesus!). A black youth from Ghana, Matthew Ayariga, not a baptized Christian, was watching and, when asked by the captors, "Are you a Christian?" he replied, "Their God is my God." He was baptized by blood when all twenty-one were beheaded. While these martyrs had most likely never heard of Pelagius and Calvin or engaged disputes over grace, and probably would not have pitted James 2 against Romans 3 on the subject of justification, they were confident that Christ can raise life eternal from dust and ash. The purpose of Lenten disciplines, not salvific in themselves but solid training for beatitude, is to train voices to join their chorus of faith. "Mortal, can these bones live?" "O Lord God, you know."

March 1, 2017

Advice to a Young Priest

The illusion of one's being perpetually young was shattered in my case recently when a publishing firm asked me to write some advice to a young priest from the perspective of an elder. For me, youth was a permanent state. I was the very youngest in my college class and, in my Anglican years, at twenty-six I was the youngest parish rector in the nation. So defensive was I about this, that at my installation I had a friend, who eventually became a U.S. senator, read for the first lesson: "Let no man despise thy youth" (1 Tim. 4:12, KJV). That was in the days of Beatle haircuts, and my self-assurance was not affirmed when one lady remarked, upon seeing me in an elaborate cope at Evensong, that I looked like the Infant of Prague.

These years later I find it difficult to recognize that I am of "a certain age" and have been asked to speak from the platform of senior experience to those younger, but that is the case and the reality, and so I can pass along some thoughts about the parish priesthood that, had I known then what I know now, would have made those years easier, but less of an adventure. I copy here a small bit of the advice I passed along to that publisher.

Characteristics of a Well-Run Parish

First of all, a good shepherd can say after the sublime model of pastors: "I know my own and my own know me" (John 10:14).

Our Peculiar Times

It is good to cultivate a gift for remembering names, and I regret that I never had that gift to cultivate to begin with. In defense, remembering faces and voices and the ups and downs of people's lives is more important. There are those who amaze others with an ability to remember names, as if it were some sort of parlor trick, but they never get behind the name. Wherever the parish is, big or small, it will have various identifiable personality types, and the good pastor will quickly identify them, remembering all the while that however attractive and helpful or dismaying and belligerent they may be, Christ died for each of them, and the pastor will be accountable for each of them on the Day of Judgment. If a parish priest is available in crises, is at sick beds and mourns with those who mourn, he will be absolved of minor disagreements with the flower guild and finance committee. If he forgets their names, what counts is that the faces of those who have departed will pass before him on the first two days of November.

This is more important than being amiable, and indeed it is the very opposite of false amiability. The "jolly good guy" kind of pastor can be an irritant. Such a caricature of agape recalls the indelible image of the happy clown on the circus midway, who is all confusion underneath. It is prudent not to equate the dignity of the sacramental office with the way a man exercises it, and it is wise indeed to be especially careful not to think that Christian joy is the same as the self-conscious jollity, and even buffoonery, with which some clerics camouflage their discomfort with the truth of Christ. Ministers of the gospel are not used-car salesmen whose heartiness is a mile wide and an inch deep. A bemused layman told me that a bishop joked with him, but turned away like a startled deer when asked an important question. The Lord Himself was betrayed with a cold kiss, and stared back with unfathomable eyes.

While the daily schedule is busy and often derailed by pastoral emergencies, preparing homilies should be a weeklong job, starting out with reflection on the forthcoming Gospel. Prayerful medita-tion is the paramount form of reparation. The Internet is a resource unique to the present generation that an older parish priest might wish he had when he began his priesthood. The real challenge is "discernment of spirits" because often there is too much informa-tion to draw on, and not all of it provides worthy insights. For some decades "storytelling" was a fad in homiletics. Surely the parables are the best stories, but grasping for illustrative images, let alone belabored humor that is not at all witty, should be avoided. The best stories are the lives of the saints and historical events. If a preacher is hard pressed, he need only relate the story of a saint. That never fails. Christ is the Lord of History, and the neglect of history in a priest's formation is one of the serious deficiencies of our time.

Looking back on my decades as a parish priest, I regret the amount of time wasted in meetings. The less the churchman knows what he is doing, the more meetings, seminars, conferences, and conventions he will summon or attend. Meetings are the opiate of the bureaucrat. They should be avoided as much as possible. A new generation, happily, has less time for these indulgences than did the members of religious orders in their decline.

As years pass, the priest begins to realize, too, how wanderlust can be a seductive kind of escapism. The current pope has said, "Avoid the scandal of being airport bishops." This applies as well to priests. The Lord calls men to "become" priests because He wants them to "be" priests. The holy Curé d'Ars spent his entire priestly life in one parish. While there is some cogency to term limits for parish priests, there is also much to be said for stability. A priest looking ahead to another parish, like a bishop with his eye on another diocese, is like an alderman aiming at a governorship, and a governor with his eyes on the White House. The man becomes so circumspect in his actions that he fears making waves, and by so doing he starts to drown. St. John Chrysostom used another maritime metaphor in his disdain for careerists when he said that if a priest trims his sails in the interest of preferment, he will not know how to be a prophet when he gets what he wanted.

The Holy Mass is the heart of the Christian life, but to be that, it must proceed from the Sacrament of Confession. With exquisite subtlety the Risen Christ prompted Peter to confess before He sent him out to offer the Eucharist to the heart of the empire. The parish priest should not let a day pass without some time in the confessional, and if no one shows up, that time can be one of prayer, and eventually the people will come. Weekly confession should be the goal for the priest himself. Often the antichrist will tempt the priest to absent the confessional for one reason or another just before a seriously burdened penitent is about to ask to be heard. Humble confessions heard in the sacred tribunal often inspire the priest beyond anything the penitent could understand. Humility is never discouraged by a good examination of conscience, for the Good Physician always has a cure for sickness of soul, be it a defect of the intellect or a weakness of will. Over the decades, I have had the great encouragement of real saints, most of them unacknowledged but a few of them already canonized. Once as a student in Rome I was running out of breath during a 7.5 km race, but I got a second wind when some friends along the street cheered us runners on. I have come to hear the voices of saints in that way many times. Sometimes we may be hearing "angels unawares" (Heb. 13:2). The Discourager is never Christ but always the antichrist. As he is haunted by God, he lurks in the holiest places in the holiest moments. I used to be rattled when he caused distractions, sometimes lurid ones, at Mass. It is permissible to curse him privately in such moments. Better yet, mock him, for mockery poisons the pride of which he is the prince.

It may not take long for the newly ordained priest to perceive that in some clerical quarters, honesty is not the instinctive culture. This is more than a defect: it is a blasphemy among those consecrated to Christ whose "word is truth" (John 17:17). I allude to this gingerly as a delicate matter, for mentioning it without qualifications risks calumny, but long experience has accustomed me to being told by churchmen of high rank things that "do not conform to the truth." That is ecclesiastical jargon for simple lying. Sometimes it is pious dishonesty in the form of falling silent when asked a direct question. A forthright cardinal told me that lying was the normal policy among those on his staff, and they simply stared at the floor when challenged. Attached to this dishonesty is the infection of gossip and envy. Brothers in Christ should nurture and promote the various talents of their fellows for the prosperity of the gospel. Such is not an untutored habit among all of the brethren. Insecurity prefers mediocrity over excellence.

The younger priests should learn first of all that these temptations are backhanded compliments by Satan, whose hatred of priests has scorched every century one way or another. In these matters it would be unrealistic to expect more of bishops than one expects of oneself. The young priest sobered by a history older than himself will remember modern bishops who were serious men: for instance, heroes in the German Church such as Michael von Faulhaber, Clemens August von Galen, Konrad von Preysing, and Josef Frings, while some others were satisfied to adjust to those barbaric times. As remedy for cynicism, it is well to remember what St. John Fisher said upon realizing that he was the only bishop in the Tudor realm willing to speak truth to power and to die for it: "The fort is betrayed even of them that should have defended it. And therefore seeing the matter is thus begun, and so faintly resisted on our parts, I fear that we be not the men that shall see the end of the misery." The parish priest will not let the timidity of some distract him from the stoic grandeur of Ignatius and Polycarp and sturdy bishops through the present years: Pierre-Marie Gerlier in the secret catacombs of Lyons, Bishop Patrick Byrne dying in the snows of Korea, and Nguyen Van Thuan isolated in a Vietnamese prison, for they are the true successors of all but one of the apostles.

Having spent years in Rome, I am immeasurably grateful for the experience, in no little measure because it sobered me with the realization that the Church's supernatural character is not understood without the revelation of her human character with both its virtues and flaws. The priest's love for the Church is rooted in sacrifice and not romanticism, lest her wrinkles and scars, as the years progress, dismay the priest's bond with the Bride of Christ. I have profited much from the words and wisdom of Ronald Knox, whom I think was the finest preacher of the twentieth century, and whose singularly original insights will rescue any priest preparing his homilies in uninspired hours, and so I have come to understand more profoundly his explanation for rarely visiting Rome: "He who travels in the Barque of Peter had better not look too closely into the engine room."

There is no flattery in God's choice of a man to act in His name. "But God hath chosen the foolish things of the world to confound the wise; and God hath chosen the weak things of the world to confound the things which are mighty" (1 Cor. 1:27, KJV). The parish priest is sent by the Lord to catch souls. As a priest gets older, he may be tempted, in the manner of fishermen, to exaggerate the size of his catch, or to regret when the net is empty. On the Last Day he cannot lie to the Righteous Judge who asks, "Children, have you caught anything?" (see John 21:5). Our reply may be barren, but we will notice with astonishment that He calls us "children," even though the world has called us "father." Then, like a burst of light, it will dawn that He is the High Priest, and we were fathers only because of His elegant condescension and delegation. He makes great beyond counting what was our very poor catch, because if we have saved one soul in all our feeble years, it will be to Him as if we had brought Him the whole world.

August 7, 2017

About the Author

Father George Rutler has long been a pastor of parishes in the heart of New York City. He holds numerous academic degrees from the United States and Europe and is the author of thirty books. He has broadcast programs on EWTN since the early 1980s.

Sophia Institute

Sophia Institute is a nonprofit institution that seeks to nurture the spiritual, moral, and cultural life of souls and to spread the Gospel of Christ in conformity with the authentic teachings of the Roman Catholic Church.

Sophia Institute Press fulfills this mission by offering translations, reprints, and new publications that afford readers a rich source of the enduring wisdom of mankind.

Sophia Institute also operates the popular online resource CatholicExchange.com. *Catholic Exchange* provides world news from a Catholic perspective as well as daily devotionals and articles that will help readers to grow in holiness and live a life consistent with the teachings of the Church.

In 2013, Sophia Institute launched Sophia Institute for Teachers to renew and rebuild Catholic culture through service to Catholic education. With the goal of nurturing the spiritual, moral, and cultural life of souls, and an abiding respect for the role and work of teachers, we strive to provide materials and programs that are at once enlightening to the mind and ennobling to the heart; faithful and complete, as well as useful and practical.

Sophia Institute gratefully recognizes the Solidarity Association for preserving and encouraging the growth of our apostolate over the course of many years. Without their generous and timely support, this book would not be in your hands.

www.SophiaInstitute.com
www.CatholicExchange.com
www.SophiaInstituteforTeachers.org